Preparing for Sunday

Preparing for Sunday

Exploring the Readings for Year B

J. E. Spicer, CSsR

NOVALIS

© 2002 Novalis, Saint Paul University, Ottawa, Canada

Cover design and layout: Suzanne Latourelle

Business Office:
Novalis
49 Front Street East, 2nd Floor
Toronto, Ontario, Canada
M5E 1B3

Phone: 1-800-387-7164 or (416) 363-3303
Fax: 1-800-204-4140 or (416) 363-9409
E-mail: cservice@novalis.ca
www.novalis.ca

National Library of Canada Cataloguing in Publication

Spicer, John (John E.)
    Preparing for Sunday : exploring the readings for year
B / John Spicer.

ISBN 2-89507-305-8

    1. Bible–Liturgical lessons, English. 2. Church year
meditations. 3. Catholic Church–Prayer-books and devotions–
English. I. Title.

BS390.S65 2002   264'.029   C2002-903743-3

Printed in Canada.

We acknowledge the financial support of the Government of
Canada through the Book Publishing Industry Development
Program (BPIDP) for our publishing activities.

Contents

Preface

Near the beginning of my priestly ministry, I gathered groups of people to reflect on our faith. I was amazed at the sense of togetherness that these groups experienced and also at the valuable insights they expressed and shared.

In 1968, Archbishop Jordan asked me to head a new commission in the Archdiocese of Edmonton: Adult Religious Education (a first in Canada). I began by writing reflection booklets on the documents of Vatican II, and then went on to produce bible reflection booklets and guidelines on Mark, Matthew, Luke/Acts, John, and Revelation. These were well received.

More recently, I wrote reflection booklets for all three cycles of Sunday readings. Groups as well as individuals in the Archdiocese found these booklets very helpful as they explore their faith.

Preparing for Sunday: Exploring the Readings for Year B grew out of these reflection booklets and will now reach a wider audience. I am convinced that readers' insights, together with those offered here, will lead many people to a deeper appreciation of the great scriptural heritage that is ours.

May God, the Father, Son and Spirit, be with you as you ponder God's word.

J.E. Spicer, CSsR
Edmonton
September 2002

Introduction

How to Use This Resource

Preparing for Sunday is a hands-on, accessible resource for people who wish to explore more deeply the readings for the coming Sunday. Each Sunday lists the readings of the day, offers a brief reflection on the readings and how they relate to our lives today, and ends with four questions.

Begin your reflection time with a prayer. Then read aloud each of the scripture readings listed. After reading my reflection, explore the four questions. If you are part of a group, you may wish to use these "points of departure" to stimulate discussion; if you are using the book on your own, you may simply reflect on the questions or write in a journal. These questions may be reworded or adapted for your setting.

The readings for each Sunday are from the Sunday Lectionary. The Sunday readings are in a three-year cycle (Year A, B and C). Each cycle begins with the first Sunday of Advent and ends with the feast of Christ the King. You will find the readings in a missal or missalette.

Welcome to *Preparing for Sunday*! May the time you spend reflecting on the Word of God bear much fruit!

First Sunday of Advent

Isaiah 63:16b-17; 64:1, 3-8
1 Corinthians 1:3-9
Mark 13:31-37

Someone to Trust In

In this day of shaky stock markets and international unrest, our hearts cry out for something or someone in whom we can put our trust. Otherwise, our lives can seem sterile, empty. But where can such trust be found? Surely not in anything material. Deep down we know that only God is worthy of our fullest trust. This beautiful truth emerges in the readings for the first Sunday of Advent.

In the first reading, Isaiah, writing after the Babylonian Exile (587–537 BCE), confidently exclaims to God: "You, O Lord, are our father; 'our Redeemer from of old' is your name." He then proceeds to pray: "O that you would tear open the heavens and come down…no ear has perceived, no eye has seen any God besides you, who works for those who wait for him." (The gospel writers use the first sentence of this latter quotation in the scene of Jesus' baptism, making it clear that Jesus is the answer to Isaiah's prayer.) The first reading concludes with a well-known text on trust: "Yet, O Lord, you are our Father; we are the clay, and you are our potter; we are all the work of your hand."

In the second reading, Paul thanks God for his Corinthian converts. God is working through them for the good of others. "I give thanks to my God always for you because of the grace of God that has been given you in Christ Jesus, for in every way you have been enriched in him…."

We, too, are gifted and graced people. The Holy Spirit opens up new ways for our various gifts to be used both within the Christian community and in the wider human community. Through each of us God reaches out to others, seeking their trust.

The gospel for this first Sunday of Advent reminds us that complete vindication of our trust in God will come only at the end-time. Concerning this time, Jesus warns us: "Therefore, keep awake – in the evening, or at midnight, or at cockcrow, or at dawn, or else he may find you asleep when he comes suddenly."

Jesus points out that we must not allow our trust in God to lie idle in the background of our lives. It is to be in the forefront. actively shaping our thoughts, words and actions. If this is true for us, then we need not fear the end-time. On the contrary, we can look forward in trust, awaiting God's warm and full embrace, just as a child looks forward to coming home, or a lover looks forward to being with the beloved.

1. Describe your experiences of trust – trusting others, and having others trust you.
2. How are you like clay in the hands of God the potter? How does this make you feel?
3. How can you "keep awake" and prepare for the end-time?
4. What word or phrase from the readings will you carry with you this week?

Second Sunday of Advent

Isaiah 40:1-5, 9-11
2 Peter 3:8-15a
Mark 1:1-8

Bogged Down?

Often we find ourselves bogged down, ready to give up. There's simply too much on our plates. Our past mistakes catch up with us; a serious misadventure or crisis looms. As a result, we become disheartened and confused. We need help.

We find it in this Sunday's readings.

In the first reading, God tells Isaiah, "Comfort, O comfort my people…. Speak tenderly to Jerusalem…she has served her term…her penalty is paid." Then, as Isaiah looks to the future, a voice cries out: "In the wilderness prepare the way of the Lord…then the glory of the Lord shall be revealed and all people shall see it together… say to the cities of Judah, 'Here is your God!'" The reading ends with these extraordinary words: "He will feed his flock like a shepherd; he will gather the lambs in his arms, and carry them in his bosom."

God is indeed a God of deliverance. God frees us, first by taking away our sins, then by opening us to a future of great promise.

In the gospel, Mark makes clear that John the Baptist fulfills the prophecy of Isaiah found in the first reading. He notes that the Baptist "appeared in the wilderness proclaiming a baptism…for the forgiveness of sins." The Baptist, however, points to the coming of another "who is more powerful than I…. I have baptized you with water; but he will baptize you with the Holy Spirit."

Jesus is thus the final deliverer. He is "the glory of the Lord." He is the shepherd "who gathers the lambs in his arms."

If, after reflecting on these two readings, we still feel hesitant about our good fortune, let us take heart from Peter's words in the second reading: "The Lord is not slow about his promise, as some think of slowness, but is patient with you, not wanting any to perish, but all to come to repentance. But the day of the Lord will come like a thief, and then the heavens will pass away.... But, in accordance with his promise, we wait for new heavens and a new earth...."

Deliverance is indeed here, but not yet fully. Hence, we journey into the future, assured that our sins are forgiven and convinced that we have an urgent task to fulfill.

1. Describe a time when you were bogged down and didn't know which way to turn.
2. How do today's readings speak to such experiences?
3. Besides finding hope and courage in the word of God, what else can you do when you are bogged down with overwhelming difficulties?
4. What word or phrase from the readings will you carry with you this week?

Third Sunday of Advent

Isaiah 61:1-2a, 10-11
I Thessalonians 5:16-24
John 1:6-8, 19-28

Do We Own Ourselves?

In medieval days, few country people owned land. Rather, from birth to death they slaved away on property belonging to others. At the end of life they had nothing to bequeath to their children except their own sad plight.

We look back with pity on such a sad state of affairs, perhaps unaware that these same conditions still exist in many developing countries. Closer to home, these conditions may also endure in our own lives, in many subtle ways.

The truth is that we still live in bondage. Through poor decisions, we put ourselves in shackles. These shackles prevent us from growing. Because we live within the false value system of modern society, we tend to become alienated from our own true selves. It can be said that we really do not fully own ourselves. Various taskmasters own us.

How can we repossess ourselves? This Sunday's readings give the answer.

In the first reading, Isaiah speaks to the Israelites, who are held in bondage during the Babylonian exile. He promises them release. Speaking of one to come he says, "The spirit of the Lord GOD is upon me, because the Lord has anointed me; he has sent me to bring good news to the oppressed, to bind up the brokenhearted, to proclaim liberty to the captives, and release to the prisoners; to proclaim the year of the Lord's favour..." [i.e., a jubilee year, when land was restored to the original owners].

This was good news indeed for the Jewish exiles. It is good news for us as well. For we, too, have broken hearts; we, too, are captives in many ways; we, too, are in prisons; and we, too, have lost much of ourselves to foreign landlords.

In the second reading, Paul advises the Thessalonians that, freed in Christ, they can now pursue a fruitful life. "Rejoice always, pray without ceasing…. Do not quench the Spirit…. hold fast to what is good; abstain from every form of evil. May the God of peace himself sanctify you entirely…. The one who calls you is faithful, and he will do this."

In the gospel, John the Baptist is portrayed as a witness to the coming light. He openly confesses, "I am not the Messiah." Rather, he is the one of whom Isaiah spoke. He is "the voice…crying out in the wilderness, 'Make straight the way of the Lord.'" He continues, "I baptize with water. Among you stands one whom you do not know, the one who is coming after me; I am not worthy to untie the thong of his sandal."

The one the Baptist refers to is Jesus. He is the one, the only one, who can release us from bondage. For he is both truly human and truly God. In him we can repossess our true selves.

1. Describe an experience that gave you new insights into who you are.
2. What does "true identity" mean?
3. What did you hear in this Sunday's readings that could help you regain your true identity as a child of God?
4. What word or phrase from the readings will you carry with you this week?

Fourth Sunday of Advent

2 Samuel 7:1-5, 8b-12, 14a,16
Romans 16:25-27
Luke 1:26-38

Promises – Ours and God's

The promises we humans make are limited by our weakness. Even though they may be made in good faith and with the best of intentions, our promises are frequently left unfulfilled and at times deliberately broken. Even our most solemn promises are not secure.

God's promises, however, are a different matter. We can rely on them absolutely. God makes two different kinds of promises. One is conditional: God promises a certain outcome if we fulfill our part of the bargain. The other is totally unconditional: it will be fulfilled no matter what. It is the latter kind of promise that the readings for this, the fourth Sunday of Advent, explore.

The first reading finds King David at a time when his most crucial battles were behind him, and he could turn his attention to other matters. It dawned on him that the Lord of Israel had only a tent. Surely he should have a temple! God, however, uses the occasion to point out that he is more interested in another kind of house. Through the prophet Nathan, God said to David, "The Lord will make you a house.... Your house and your kingdom shall be made sure forever before me; your throne shall be established forever."

This is an unconditional promise. God will build a house for David that will last forever.

The second reading tells us how God fulfilled his promise to David. Paul tells the Romans that the good news he preaches is "the proclamation of Jesus Christ, ...that was kept secret for long ages but is now disclosed...is made known to all the Gentiles...to bring about the obedience of faith – to the only wise God, through Jesus Christ, to whom be the glory forever! Amen."

The gospel reading is Luke's account of the Annunciation. The angel Gabriel is sent to tell Mary that she will conceive and bear a son who "will be called the Son of the Most High, and the Lord God will give to him the throne of his ancestor David. He will reign over the house of Jacob forever, and of his kingdom there will be no end."

Mary replies, "Here am I, the servant of the Lord; let it be with me according to your word."

God's unconditional promise to David is thus fulfilled – wonderfully fulfilled! Though indeed unconditional, note that God waited upon a positive response from Mary. She gave it. And that is a sign to us. God's promise of a house that will last forever is still being fulfilled in our time. It awaits our response. Like Mary, let us respond positively, thus taking part in the coming of the kingdom.

1. Describe a time when a promise that you made (or that others made to you) was fulfilled or unfulfilled.

2. How was God's promise to David fulfilled by Jesus?

3. How do you see yourself as being part of God's answer to David? How do you take part in the unfolding of God's kingdom?

4. What word or phrase from the readings will you carry with you this week?

Christmas

Mass During the Night

Isaiah 9:2-4, 6-7
Titus 2:11-14
Luke 2:1-16

Mass at Dawn

Isaiah 62:11-12
Titus 3:4-7
Luke 2:15-20

Mass During the Day

Isaiah 52:7-10
Hebrews 1:1-6
John 1:1-18

There's More to It Than Meets the Eye

All too often we miss the central point of a story. All too often we fail to catch the real beauty of a scene. And all too often we fail to recognize the deeper implications of an event. We are preoccupied with many relatively unimportant things. As hustle-and-bustle people, we rush by when we should pause. We keep looking around instead of centring our gaze.

Christmas is an exciting time. There's so much tinsel about, so much decoration. There are so many people to greet, so many gifts to give and receive. Thus the heart of Christmas becomes obscured.

The heart of Christmas is, of course, Christ. But the newborn Christ is not the focus of the infancy narratives of Matthew and Luke. They use the infant to portray the man, the man who is truly Messiah, Saviour and Lord. Both evangelists take great pains to show that Jesus comes into the world in order to fulfill the long-held expectations about the coming Messiah.

Moreover, they foreshadow in their infancy stories the important aspects of Jesus' adult life, particularly his suffering, death and resurrection.

There is far more meaning to the Christmas crib than we allow. There is far more beauty in it than we have imagined. And there are far greater implications in it for our daily lives that we have yet to discover.

Christmas indeed gives us a glimpse into the profound mystery of incarnation. Matthew and Luke masterfully introduce us to it. May our Christmas prayer and wish be that all of us, as we pause before the crib, will slowly drink in the rich nourishment it so bountifully offers.

To all a Merry Christmas and a Happy New Year.

1. In the first reading, Isaiah foresees the birth of one who will free Israel. What makes this reading so rich?*

2. In the second reading, Paul writes to his companion, Titus, about the richness given us in Jesus. Reflect on his words.

3. Luke's words in the gospel for Midnight Mass are among the most majestic and powerful in the Bible. Share your thoughts and feelings on this reading.

4. What word or phrase from the readings will you carry with you this week?

* Note: These questions refer to the readings from Midnight Mass.

Holy Family

Genesis 15:1-6; 17:3b-5, 15-16; 21:1-7
Hebrews 11:8, 11-12, 17-19
Luke 2:22-40

Roots

Without roots there would be no trees, no vegetables, no flowers. Thrust deep into the soil, roots supply needed nourishment. As human beings we also have roots. And what could our deepest roots possibly be if not our families?

In a healthy family we receive much nourishment – a sense of belonging, a sense of our own worth. In the family we also learn how to love, how to get along with others and many other important things. It is this family experience that nourishes us and makes possible our fruitful living in larger communities – our neighbourhood, our town or city, our nation, our world.

Any help to families, therefore, is good news. We find such help in this Sunday's readings for the feast of the Holy Family.

In the first reading, childless Abram and Sarai, though advanced in age, are assured by God that they will have descendants. (Sarai is so amazed, she bursts out laughing!) Now they will have someone to inherit their property. But such a blessing was small compared to the future God promised. Abram was to become the ancestor of all the nations of the world. Such a destiny called for new names: Abraham and Sarah.

The second reading is based on the first. The author of Hebrews praises Abraham for his deep faith in God. Then he re-emphasizes that Abraham's descendants would indeed be "as many as the stars of

23

heaven and as the innumerable grains of sand by the seashore."

In the gospel reading we learn just how God intended to fulfill the promise made to Abraham. When the child Jesus was brought to Jerusalem for presentation to the Lord, the holy man Simeon, taking Jesus in his arms and looking up to heaven, said, "…my eyes have seen your salvation, which you have prepared in the presence of all peoples, a light for revelation to the Gentiles and for glory to your people Israel."

Indeed, as the gospel says, "The child grew and became strong, filled with wisdom; and the favour of God was upon him." It was in and through Jesus that God fulfilled the promise made to Abraham – that all peoples of the world would be blessed.

Through our roots in the risen Jesus, we are enabled and privileged to extend God's blessing to all the peoples in our world today.

1. Why do we all need to be "rooted" in a family?
2. How does Abraham's faith benefit us? (Paul, in Romans 4:3, quotes this sentence from Genesis: "Abram believed God, and it was reckoned to him as righteousness." Righteousness is a right relationship with God and neighbour, and the universe, a life-giving relationship.)
3. Through Jesus, God fulfills his promise to Abraham. How do we share in this promise?
4. What word or phrase from the readings will you carry with you this week?

Mary, Mother of God (January 1)

Numbers 6:22-27
Galatians 4:4-7
Luke 2:16-21

"How-to"

On the bookstore shelves today you'll find no end of "how-to" books – how to build, how to fix, how to save, how to use your computer. As helpful as these books may be, we humans have a much greater need – how to be fully human. This Sunday's readings answer this need.

First, we need God's blessing. We need it for any enterprise, but we especially need it to become the kind of people God meant us to be. We already have this blessing. It is spelled out for us beautifully in the first reading for this feast day: "The Lord bless you and keep you...."

The second reading is more specific. To be truly human, we are to be one with Christ. Earlier in Galatians, Paul says that as children "we were enslaved to the elemental spirits of the world." In today's reading he goes on to say that "God sent his Son, born of a woman...in order to redeem those who were under the law, so that we might receive adoption as children." Only as children of God can we become fully human.

Mary, whose motherhood we celebrate today, has much help to offer us. When the angel Gabriel, in God's name, invited her to be the mother of "the son of the Most High," Mary replied, "...let it be with me according to your word." By this reply Mary teaches us to have faith in God. Such faith is the basis of becoming truly human.

Luke's gospel reading for the feast of Mary teaches another indispensable way of becoming more fully human. After the angels and shepherds had left Bethlehem, "Mary treasured all these words and pondered them in her heart."

Later on, when Jesus had entered upon his public life, Mary surely treasured her son's teachings and pondered them. At Cana, for instance, Mary said to the servants, "Do what he tells you."

To grow to the fullness of our humanity we, too, must treasure and ponder the words Jesus spoke. We, too, like the servants at Cana, must do what Jesus tells us to do.

On this feast of Mary, Mother of God, we are most grateful to her for the help she gives us on "how to" become more fully human.

1. Describe a time when you learned how to perform a particular task.
2. Jesus is the "only begotten Son of God." But we are adopted children of God, as Paul tells us in the second reading. What does this adoption mean to you?
3. Put yourself in Mary's place. How do you think she felt being the mother of Jesus?
4. How does Mary help us become more fully human?

Epiphany

Isaiah 60:1-6
Ephesians 3:2-3a, 5-6
Matthew 2:1-12

"Hitch Your Wagon to a Star"

Ralph Waldo Emerson, the great American writer, is the author of this phrase, but its roots are in the early days of western settlement. To keep their covered wagons on course when travelling by night, the pioneers kept their eyes on a particular star.

To be on course in life is a challenge for all of us. But what is the right course? How can we stay on course? These are the important questions. Christians have a true, unfailing star to help us in our journey, as the readings for this feast of the Epiphany make clear.

In the first reading, Isaiah heralds the dawning of a new day for Israel. "Arise, shine, for your light has come, and the glory of the Lord has risen upon you!" Darkness covers the earth, but for Israel, "The Lord will arise upon you.... Nations shall come to your light."

In the second reading, Paul tells his Ephesian converts that "the Gentiles have become fellow heirs, members of the same body, and sharers in the promise in Christ Jesus through the gospel."

What God promised through Abraham and Isaiah has now, in Jesus, come to fulfillment.

The gospel reading makes this fulfillment in Jesus even more clear. Wise men came from the East looking for the child whose star they had seen "at its rising." Advised by the cunning Herod (but unaware of his hidden agenda), they travelled to Bethlehem, where "they saw the child with Mary his mother...they knelt down and paid him homage." Warned in a dream, they did not return to Herod but went to their own country.

God works slowly, but ever so surely! Long awaited, the Son of God was born as one of us, like us in all things except sin (though he took upon himself our sinfulness). In living out his humanity he became our guiding star. Throughout our lives we meet others who help and guide us, but we must judge such help and guidance in light of the person and teaching of Jesus. He, and he alone, is "the way, and the truth and the life." In him and through him we will remain on course to our journey's end – eternal life.

1. Describe how you went about setting goals in your life and how you pursued those goals.
2. How do the three readings of this feast day help you focus on the true purpose of life?
3. How do the readings help you pursue this purpose?
4. What word or phrase from the readings will you carry with you this week?

Baptism of the Lord

Isaiah 55:1-11
1 John 5:1-9
Mark 1:7-11

Getting Your Feet Wet

How often we hesitate to get our feet wet! We resist trying something new. Old ways of thinking and acting are good enough, thank you!

Certainly we need to exercise caution before stepping into the new. But accept the new we must, for the new is happening all the time – in the world of science, in the world of technology, indeed, in all fields of human endeavour. It's also happening in our own lives. The readings for this Sunday, Baptism of the Lord, help us to come to terms with this fact.

In the first reading, Isaiah invites us to "Come to the waters." He goes on to say, "Why do you spend your money for that which is not bread?" Then he tells us what is truly bread for us: "Seek the Lord while he may be found, call upon him while he is near." Isaiah concludes by assuring us that just as the rain and snow bring about abundant crops, so God's word will "accomplish that which I purpose...."

In the second reading, John poses this powerful question: "Who is it that conquers the world but the one who believes that Jesus is the Son of God?"

Jesus is the most wonderful new thing that has ever happened in human history. Through his life, death and resurrection, he conquered the world – not by the sword, but by love. Hence, those who believe in Jesus and live out that belief are extending the victory of Jesus. They are discovering new vistas and opening new doors. They are helping themselves and others to ever-new beginnings.

In the gospel reading, the Baptist points to one who "will baptize you with the Holy Spirit." This Spirit leads us onwards in our pilgrimage to God, a pilgrimage that reveals an ever-deepening faith. Thus we are called upon daily to leave the past behind and travel into the future, towards the "new heavens and new earth."

What an exciting invitation!

1. When have you had to leave the past behind and embrace the future? Describe one of these experiences.
2. Think about Isaiah's invitation to "Come to the waters…. Seek the Lord while he may be found." How do these words make you feel?
3. In the second reading, John asks, "Who is it that conquers the world but the one who believes that Jesus is the Son of God?" What does this mean for you?
4. We are all baptized with the Holy Spirit. What does such a baptism mean in your life?

Second Sunday in Ordinary Time

1 Samuel 3:3b-10, 19
1 Corinthians 6:13c-15a, 17-20
John 1:35-42

Emmanuel (God with Us)

Sometimes we may be tempted to look at our lives and say, "What's the point?" We are busy, yes, but seem to be going nowhere, at least nowhere worthwhile. And who cares anyway? Perhaps a few people who are close to us care. But most people would not give it much thought if we faded out of the picture, we may say to ourselves.

So goes the temptation. But a temptation it is. For our life isn't pointless. Others do need us, and they profit by our presence. More importantly, God has his eyes on us. We are part of his dream for humanity. This truth is made clear in the readings for this coming Sunday.

In the first reading, God called to Samuel, who was lying down in the temple. Samuel thought it was Eli who called him. But Eli said it wasn't. The same voice came to Samuel a second and a third time. By then Eli realized that it was God calling. So he told Samuel that when he heard the voice again he was to say, "Speak, Lord, for your servant is listening." The reading ends, "As Samuel grew up, the Lord was with him and let none of his words fall to the ground."

Because Samuel was attentive to God's voice, God remained with him. And because God was with him, people listened to him. He had a great influence on many lives.

The second reading makes the point that when, like Samuel, we hear the voice of God, our entire self, body and soul, is to be at God's service. The Greeks of Corinth did not see the importance of the body. It was only a passing reality, or so they thought. Thus for someone to have relations with a prostitute was a minor peccadillo. Not so, says Paul: "Or do you not know that your body is a temple of the Holy Spirit within you, which you have from God, and that you are not your own? For you were bought with a price; therefore glorify God in your body."

Because we are called to God's service, our entire being, body and soul, belongs to God.

The gospel reading also shows how each one of us fits into God's plan. John the Baptist points to Jesus and says to two of his own group, "Look, here is the Lamb of God!" The two go to Jesus and ask, "Rabbi, where are you staying?" "Come and see," Jesus replies. So they went with him "and remained with him that day."

One of the two who remained with Jesus was named Andrew. The next day he told his brother Simon what had happened to him. "We have found the Messiah!" he said. Simon then went with him to see Jesus. Looking hard at Simon, Jesus said, "You are Simon son of John. You are to be called Cephas (which is translated Peter [and means 'rock'])."

Andrew was thus instrumental in having his brother, now called Peter, join Christ. We all know how important Peter was in the early Church. So it is with all of us. Our lives in Christ are anything but pointless. Each life of faith is an integral part of God's loving design for all creation.

During the Christmas season we frequently hear the word "Emmanuel." It means "God with us." God is indeed with us and for us.

1. Talk about times when you have felt that your life was pointless.
2. We all want to be wanted. How do the readings for this Sunday help you realize how much God wants you?
3. What do you think is God's overall plan for us and for our universe?
4. How does knowing how important you are in God's eyes affect your daily life? What changes will you make as a result?

Third Sunday in Ordinary Time

Jonah 3:1-5, 10
1 Corinthians 7:29-31
Mark 1:14-20

About-turn

Many years ago, a college teacher gave our class the task of writing an essay entitled "If Youth But Knew What Age Could Tell." I haven't a clue what I wrote at the time. But I'm sure my thoughts would be very different now.

It seems to be human nature that it takes us a long time to get to the heart of the matter. We first poke around with many side issues. But time is precious. So sacred Scripture keeps reminding us of our main purpose in life. This Sunday's readings are a good example of such reminders.

The first reading has to do with the rather comic figure of Jonah. Reluctant to go where God wanted, he was, willy-nilly, transported thither in the belly of a whale. When he landed on the shore God commanded him a second time, "Get up, go to Nineveh, that great city, and proclaim to it the message that I tell you."

Jonah dragged himself off to do as he had been bidden. To the Ninevites he announced, "Forty days more, and Nineveh shall be overthrown!" On hearing this message the Ninevites "believed God; they proclaimed a fast.... God changed his mind about the calamity that he had said he would bring upon them; and he did not do it."

In the second reading, Paul points out to his Corinthian converts that "the appointed time has grown short." He continues, "For the present form of this world is passing away."

34

The gospel reading, from the first chapter of Mark, tells us that Jesus said to all his hearers, "The time is fulfilled and the kingdom of God has come near; repent and believe in the good news." Then he called Andrew and Simon, James and John to be his disciples. They immediately left their work and possessions and followed him.

The good news of the gospel is that God calls us, in and through Jesus, to an ever-growing participation in divine life. Only in God can we find fullfillment. This is a central truth of faith. It demands of us full repentance, a complete about-turn. This means that we must view all things from a new perspective. Following Jesus comes first; everything else is secondary.

Like the Ninevites of the first reading, like Paul in his message to the Corinthians, and like the disciples in the gospel, we must recognize the nature of time and give God's call top priority.

1. Have you ever taken a long time to face one of life's challenges? Describe your experience.
2. What lessons do you find in the Jonah story?
3. What does Paul mean when he says, "the present form of this world is passing away"?
4. Reflect on Jesus' words in Mark's gospel: "The time is fulfilled and the kingdom of God is close at hand; repent and believe the good news."

Fourth Sunday in Ordinary Time

Deuteronomy 18:15-20
1 Corinthians 7:17, 32-35
Mark 1:21-28

Speaking Our Minds

Most people do not hesitate to speak their minds when the occasion calls for it. Parents, for instance, unhesitatingly correct their children. Husbands and wives speak out whenever the welfare of the other is concerned. Friends do the same.

Of course it isn't always easy to speak our minds. Still, much good can come from doing so. At the very least it clears the air.

We take such daily "speaking out" in stride. But we hesitate when it comes to speaking out in God's name. That's because we have almost forgotten our prophetic calling. In Baptism we were anointed to be prophets. What does this mean? This Sunday's readings help us understand.

In the first reading, Moses says to the people, "The Lord your God will raise up for you a prophet like me from among your own people; you shall heed such a prophet." Moses was thinking of those who would succeed him as God's witnesses. The first Christians, however, knew these words applied in a special way to Jesus.

In the second reading, Paul, speaking to those who are unmarried, advises them to remain as they were. The end-time, in his mind, was close at hand. Besides, as single people, they could devote more time to the affairs of God. This wasn't a popular thing to say, but Paul said it anyway.

In the gospel, Jesus gives his first public address, on the Sabbath in the synagogue at Capernaum. The congregation was astounded at his teaching, "for he taught them as one having authority."

In the audience was a man possessed of an unclean spirit. He called Jesus "the Holy One of God." But Jesus said sharply, "Be silent, and come out of him!" and the unclean spirit did so. The people were amazed. They did not realize that Jesus was *the* prophet to come, the prophet of the end-time.

It is into this line of prophets that you and I have been baptized. (We are all "prophets, priests and kings," as Scripture says.) How are we to respond to this baptismal heritage?

First, we must accept that our baptism is indeed a challenge to speak in God's name. Jesus said, "Go therefore and make disciples of all nations...." These words are addressed to all followers within his community.

Second, to fulfill our prophetic role, we must put on the mind and heart of Jesus, for as prophets we are to speak in his name, not our own.

Once we are immersed in the wisdom and love of Jesus, we are to speak out as the occasion demands and the Spirit moves. This won't always be easy. But it can be done. For God speaks through us despite our shortcomings, hesitations and misgivings.

1. How do you feel about "speaking your mind"?
2. Prominent Christians are sometimes described as "prophets." What can help you remember that you are a prophet, too?
3. What should you keep in mind as you exercise your prophetic ministry?
4. What word or phrase from the readings will you carry with you this week?

Fifth Sunday in Ordinary Time

Job 7:1-4, 6-7
1 Corinthians 9:16-19, 22-23
Mark 1:29-39

A Coin Has Two Sides

A coin has two sides; so does life. On one side, life is day-to-day drudgery, full of failed dreams and shattered hopes. On the other side, life contains moments of joy, peace and a sense of purpose. These moments may not come often, but they still keep us plugging along through the challenging days, allowing us to hope against hope that things will turn out well. Maybe, just maybe, we think, our dreams are not in vain.

This Sunday's readings examine both sides of the coin, but leave us with no doubt about upon which side to base our lives.

In the first reading, Job touches unerringly upon every phase of life's dark side. For instance, he asks, "Do not human beings have a hard service on earth, and are not their days like the days of a labourer?" He goes on, "...so I am allotted months of emptiness, and nights of misery...my eye will never again see good." Not a glimmer of light enters into this picture that Job so honestly paints. And yet, he never loses faith in God.

The two other readings look at the other side of the coin.

In the second reading, Paul describes to the Corinthians how he sees his preaching of the gospel. He desires no pay for this work. His reward is simply to be able to offer "the gospel free of charge," even though in doing so he made himself "a slave to all."

But as he says, it's all worth it in order "that I may share in its blessings."

In the gospel, Mark tells us how Jesus healed Simon Peter's mother-in-law and other great numbers of sick and possessed people. So great were the numbers cured that his companions wanted him to stay on the spot, for, as they said, "Everyone is searching for you." But Jesus answered, "Let us go on to the neighbouring towns, so that I may proclaim the message there also; for that is what I came out to do." Obviously Jesus is "good news."

All of our lives contain some drudgery and sorrow, but in Christ, all drudgery and sorrow become the birth pangs of new life. In basing our lives on Christ, our pain, taken in faith, becomes part of our journey as it was part of Christ's journey. Our sorrows become balanced by the conviction that a new day is dawning, an everlasting day when we will live forever in God's loving embrace.

∽❀∼

1. Describe some of your failed dreams and shattered hopes.
2. How is your experience of failure like what Job went through in the first reading? How is your experience different from Job's?
3. In the second reading, Paul says that he preaches the gospel so that he may participate in its blessings. What blessings is he referring to?
4. How do you see Jesus as "good news" – indeed, the best of news?

Sixth Sunday in Ordinary Time

Leviticus 13:1-2, 45-46
1 Corinthians 10:23–11:1
Mark 1:40-45

Would You Touch a Leper?

Few of us have ever met a leper, nor are we likely to do so, for relatively few people today have this affliction, which is now known as Hansen's disease.

So why am I asking you about lepers? Because there are lepers of all kinds around us – the marginalized, the outcast, the hopeless, the underprivileged, the "no accounts." These are the lepers of our society. There are too many of them to count. And what about the darkness within ourselves? This, too, is a kind of leprosy. Who will touch and cure us? This Sunday's readings answer this question.

In the first reading, Moses commands that those suspected of having leprosy be brought before the priests, who will judge whether these individuals have the disease. If they do have leprosy, they are to be excluded from the community, regarded as "unclean" and unfit to take part in the public rituals. This seems like a harsh way to treat lepers. But for that time, when few effective medicines were available, it was the only way the people could protect themselves from contagion. When Jesus came, however, he brought about a change of attitude.

In the gospel, a leper came up to Jesus (that's how approachable he was!) and said, "If you choose, you can make me clean." Jesus felt sorry for him, stretched out his hand, touched him, and said, "I do choose. Be made clean!" At once the leper was made whole. (How comforting for us in our inner sickness!)

Jesus came to bring in God's reign, a reign that is open to everyone, even to the greatest outcasts of Jesus' time – lepers. For God loves all humanity. No one is excluded from God's love. Jesus touches the leper so that we might learn to reach out and touch everyone around us, even the most despised of our society. We are appointed to "touch" such people in a variety of ways so that they may learn how worthwhile they truly are.

As we carry out this role of healing, Paul has some helpful words for us. In the second reading he says, "Give no offence to Jews or to Greeks or to the church of God, just as I try to please everyone in everything I do, not seeking my own advantage, but that of many, so that they may be saved. Be imitators of me, as I am of Christ."

Paul reached out to everyone he met, even to the poorest and most neglected of his day. In the same way, we are invited to reach out and touch even the most alienated of our own day, and to let them touch us. In doing so we are following in Jesus' footsteps.

1. How do you feel about the outcasts of our world? When was the last time you reached out to someone who is an outcast?

2. How is our own inner darkness a kind of leprosy?

3. Imagine yourself in Jesus' day. You are a leper, hidden away from society. You hear about Jesus and approach him to be cured. He cures you. What are you thinking? What are you feeling?

4. How does Jesus cure us today of our inner leprosy? How can we help cure others?

Seventh Sunday in Ordinary Time

Isaiah 43:18-19, 20-22, 24-25
2 Corinthians 1:18-22
Mark 2:1-12

Sin Is Not a Dead End!

"Repetition," the saying goes, "is the best teacher." Nowhere is this principle better exemplified than in the sacred scriptures. And in matters dealt with by the sacred writers, nowhere is repetition used more than in telling us about God's loving mercy.

The Scriptures constantly assure us of God's mercy even when we turn away from God through serious sin. God knows the hopeless feeling that such sin brings, as well as the scars it leaves within us. So God hurries to tell us how precious we are in his sight despite our deformity. God wants us to know that his mercy has far more power to heal than sin has to wound.

Last Sunday's readings, which centred on the theme of leprosy, helped us see that God has the power to heal such an affliction. This Sunday's readings go further: they speak to us of inner healing.

In the first reading, God says to us, through the prophet Isaiah, "Do not remember the former things…. I am about to do a new thing…do you not perceive it?"

We are inclined to think that what is done is done and cannot be undone. In human terms, that is true. But God is not like us. God can undo the past and open up new ways. As the first reading concludes, "I am he who blots out your transgressions…I will not remember your sins." Only a merciful God could speak in such a way!

In the second reading, Paul makes clear that all God's past promises are perfectly fulfilled in Christ, "For in him every one of God's promises is a 'Yes.'" Paul continues, "But it is God who establishes us with you in Christ...." Thus, in Christ, God's healing love and great deeds on our behalf come to fullness.

The gospel reading illustrates this consoling truth of God's forgiveness in Christ. When a paralyzed man is brought to Jesus, Jesus says, "Son, your sins are forgiven." He first cures the heart, for sin is far more tragic than lifeless limbs. But when the scribes accuse him of blasphemy (because he forgave sins – something only God could do), Jesus says, "Which is easier, to say to the paralyzed man, 'Your sins are forgiven,' or to say, 'Stand up, and take your mat, and walk'?" Then Jesus, to show his power over sin, cures the man of his physical paralysis.

What consoling readings! And so timely! For Lent will soon be upon us. As you go on to share your reflections, keep in mind the psalm's refrain: "Lord, heal my soul for I have sinned against you." Such a plea opens up to us the floodgates of God's endless, loving mercy.

1. Describe a time when you were forgiven by someone you hurt. How did being forgiven affect your relationship with that person?
2. How does God blot out our transgressions and accomplish "a new thing" within us?
3. How do you see Jesus as being God's "yes" to all God's promises?
4. Jesus cured the paralyzed man. What does this story of healing mean to you?

Eighth Sunday in Ordinary Time

Hosea 2:14, 15, 19-20
2 Corinthians 3:1-6
Mark 2:18-22

Forever Faithful

One of the great tragedies of our day is the increasing number of broken marriages. The faithful love of husband and wife is at the very centre of human life. When such love fails, the hearts of spouses are severely wounded. All of society suffers as well.

Why is marital breakdown becoming so common? There are many reasons – economic, cultural, social, psychological. This Sunday's readings point to a very basic reason why marriages fail, a reason we seldom consider.

In the first reading, the prophet Hosea, who had experienced the tragedy of a broken marriage, proclaims, "The Lord says this: ...I will take you for my wife forever; I will take you for my wife in righteousness and in justice, in steadfast love, and in mercy. I will take you for my wife in faithfulness; and you shall know the Lord."

What wonderful words! God takes us to himself as a bridegroom takes his bride: "I will take you for my wife," God says to us. And it will be forever. God does not go back on his promises. God is faithful.

Note, too, that God says, "You shall know the Lord." Married to God, we come to know him more and more. Knowing God more, we will better know ourselves, and thus will be able to grow to be fully human.

Though God is forever faithful, we are not. We are weak and fickle. Does this unfaithfulness of ours spell doom to our marriage with God? Not unless we let it. The psalm for this Sunday assures us that "The Lord is merciful and gracious, slow to anger and abounding in steadfast love. He does not deal with us according to our sins, nor repay us according to our iniquities."

In the second reading, Paul tells the Corinthians that they are his letter, a letter that is known and read by everyone. Christ himself has written in them, not with ink but with the Spirit of the living God.

Through and in Christ we are married to God. He is the bridegroom, we are the bride. That is why in the gospel, Mark quotes Jesus as saying that as long as the bridegroom is present with his friends, they cannot fast amidst the rejoicing.

So here we have the basic reason for today's marital breakdowns: we have all but forgotten our espousal to God. In Christ, through the Spirit, we are truly married to him. If we really believed this, Christian marriages could not help but be lasting and fruitful.

1. What are your thoughts on the issue of marital breakdown today? How can today's couples strengthen their sacramental bond?
2. Reflect on God's daring revelation that he is the groom and we are his bride.
3. How does Jesus bring ultimate fulfillment to our marriage with God?
4. How can we better accept ourselves as God's spouse?

Ninth Sunday in Ordinary Time

Deuteronomy 5:12-15
2 Corinthians 4:6-11
Mark 2:23–3:6

Liberation

Liberation can mean a lot of things. In a true sense, our entire lives are meant to be a process of becoming ever more free. We humans, however, have the tendency to create new ways of captivity. We are in constant need of liberation! God continually rescues us from our self-made prisons. The readings for this Sunday bear out this consoling truth.

Take the first reading. It's from the Book of Deuteronomy, a book that takes a second look at the times of Moses. Among other things, it reminds the people of God to keep the Sabbath holy. The original reason for that law was that God rested on that day; therefore, so should we. But Deuteronomy sees another reason for keeping the Sabbath day holy. "Remember that you were a slave in the land of Egypt, and the Lord your God brought you out from there…therefore the Lord your God commanded you to keep the sabbath day." The people of God thus had an added reason for keeping the Sabbath day holy: a God-given liberation.

Paul, too, in his letter to the Corinthians, speaks of liberation, a liberation brought about by Christ Jesus. "For it is the God who said, 'Let light shine out of darkness,' who has shone in our hearts to give the light of the knowledge of the glory of God in the face of Jesus Christ." Then Paul goes on to list all the times he had been held captive and how, through the courts, he was freed from them.

The gospel is also about the Sabbath day. In Jesus' day, many rules surrounding Sabbath observance were more imprisoning than liberating. For example, you were forbidden to pluck corn on the Sabbath and peel it for eating. Jesus overrode such a rule. It was also forbidden to cure the sick on the Sabbath. Jesus cured the man with a withered arm to make clear that the true meaning of the Sabbath was one of liberation.

Hence, the true meaning of the Sunday observance is that of an ever-greater freedom. Through the death and resurrection of Jesus we are freed from the many shackles that bind us. Being freed, we can love God and our neighbour fully and in ever-new ways.

1. Describe a time when you were in a bind and how you were freed from it.
2. Give examples of how we humans are good at getting into prisons of our own making.
3. Reflect on how Vatican II freed us from limits of our own making by reminding us that we are all celebrants of the Eucharist, that all people are loved and saved by God, and that "the signs of the times" are also ways of recognizing God's will for us.
4. In light of the previous question, reflect on the phrase "free to be."

First Sunday of Lent

Genesis 9:8-15
I Peter 3:18-22
Mark 1:12-15

On Being Married to God

Boy meets girl. Each discovers a new world in the other. Each gradually emerges from the smallness of self. Finally, they are ready to commit themselves to one another in the marriage covenant. In this covenant they continue their journey of discovery.

This is humanity's oldest story. It is still being told over and over again. And each telling is cause for new celebration.

What we do not always recognize is that this same story is also the story of God's relationship with us. In creation God called us to himself. But we were poor listeners and slow learners. Only bit by bit did we respond to God's advances, and our responses were weak and not always faithful. Finally, God, through Isaiah the prophet, made clear that our relationship with him was a marriage relationship.

The Bible is the story of God's love for us and our response to that love. God reaches out to us, frees us from our imprisonment, and then enters into a marriage covenant with us. The readings for this first Sunday of Lent have to do with this love relationship between God and humanity.

In the first reading, God says to Noah and his offspring, "I am establishing my covenant with you and your descendants after you...never again shall all flesh be cut off by the waters of a flood.... I have set my bow in the clouds, and it shall be a sign of the covenant between me and the earth."

The second and third readings relate to another covenant: the new and final covenant between God and humanity. To complete his wooing, God comes to us in the person of his Son. And that Son takes on our flesh. He becomes human.

In the second reading, Peter says, "Christ suffered for sins once for all, the righteous for the unrighteous, in order to bring you to God." As a sign of this new covenant, Jesus chose the waters of baptism. Through baptism we enter fully into the new covenant.

In the gospel, after being tempted in the wilderness (just as the chosen people had been tempted), Jesus triumphs over Satan (whereas our faith ancestors failed). Jesus then proclaims, "The time is fulfilled, and the kingdom of God has come near; repent, and believe in the good news."

In Jesus, the kingdom of God is close at hand. Our marriage to God has entered a new and final stage. To this happy event, indeed the happiest of all events, we respond by "repenting." That is, we change our lives completely. For we are now wedded to God in Christ through the Spirit. We are in the warm embrace of God's gentle arms. This truth is meant to pervade our whole lives and give them eternal meaning.

1. Describe someone you met on life's journey who helped you to grow.
2. How do you react to God's desire to make a marriage covenant with us? (Isaiah, in God's name, said, "I am the groom; you are the bride.")
3. How has Jesus consummated our union with God?
4. What word or phrase from the readings will you carry with you this week?

Second Sunday of Lent

Genesis 22:1-2, 9-13, 15-18
Romans 8:31b-35, 37
Mark 9:2-10

A Matter of Trust

Without trust, we humans could not live together. When we trust, our lives are enriched; when we betray trust, our lives are shattered.

The idea of trust leads us into this Sunday's readings. They emphasize, as the entire Bible does, that God alone is worthy of our full and ultimate trust. God alone will never let us down. Never.

In the first reading, Abraham, at God's bidding, is ready to sacrifice his beloved son, Isaac. At the last moment the angel of the Lord says, "Do not lay your hand on the boy or do anything to him; for now I know that you fear God."

In all likelihood, this story was originally told to deter the Jewish people from participating in the pagan practice of child sacrifice. Later generations, however, saw in it a lesson of trust in God. That is why the angel appeared a second time to reveal God's promise to Abraham: "Because you have done this...I will indeed bless you, and I will make your offspring as numerous as the stars of heaven and as the sand that is on the seashore."

Abraham's trust in God was thus fully rewarded. For God never goes back on his unconditional promises. And the promise he made to Abraham was just that – unconditional. You and I, and all Christians, are beneficiaries of this promise to Abraham. We are all witnesses to its fulfillment.

In the second reading, Paul says to the Romans, "If God is for us, who is against us? He who did not withhold his own Son...will he not with him also give us everything else?" Paul stresses the rewards of trusting in God. If we trust God, we need not fear. Even if enemies were to put us to death, God would raise us up, as he raised up his Son. God, and only God, has the final say.

The gospel continues to emphasize this point. Jesus had just told his followers about his forthcoming suffering and death. They did not understand why he had to suffer and die. But Jesus knew that, come what may, his Father would vindicate his trust. To foreshadow the ultimate triumph of God's kingdom, Jesus is transfigured before Peter, James and John. And God did vindicate Jesus' trust by raising him from the dead.

The central point of these readings is that even the worst news becomes, through trust in God, part of the good news. Life has many loose ends, many that are hard to understand and even more difficult to endure. We may never be able to tie up these loose ends, but they will ultimately make sense because of our trust in God. The gracious self-gift of God, coming to completion in eternity, will crown our trust in a way we cannot even imagine.

1. Describe a time when your trust was justified or betrayed. How did you feel?
2. How are we Christians beneficiaries of God's promise to Abraham? How are we witnesses to it?
3. Reflect on Paul's words to the Romans: "If God is for us, who is against us?"
4. Do you receive comfort from the gospel reading? How does it help you?

Third Sunday of Lent

Exodus 20:1-17
I Corinthians 1:18, 22-25
John 2:13-25

The Last Place You Thought to Look

Think about times you have lost something and, after looking high and low, finally discovered it. Perhaps you said to yourself, "That's the last place I thought of looking for it!" Keep this experience in mind as you reflect on the readings for this, the third Sunday of Lent.

The first reading is about the Ten Commandments, which God gave to us through Moses to offer guidance on life's journey. In creating us, God wrote these commandments deep in our consciousness. But we are a selfish people. We are more concerned about ourselves and our immediate needs than we are about discovering God. As a consequence, God's signposts in our hearts become faded and hard to read.

The other two readings make clear that the Ten Commandments were but the beginning of our way to God. Something more was needed if we were to mature in our knowledge and love of God. The last place God's people thought of looking for a key to this mature growth was a cross. But a cross, as it turned out, was the key.

In the second reading, Paul says with great clarity, "For Jews demand signs and Greeks desire wisdom, but we proclaim Christ crucified...." The Jews wanted to see spectacular signs before they put their faith in Jesus. Their ears were closed to his words; their eyes were closed to his miracles. The Greeks, on the other hand, wanted more and more words to match with their own wisdom. But neither spectacular deeds nor words of wisdom were enough to wake people up to the truth about Jesus. Only the cross could do it.

Paul realized that the cross was absolutely central for understanding Jesus. Only through the cross could we understand the depth of our sin and the depth of Jesus' love for us. So even though the cross was "a stumbling block" to the Jews and "foolishness" to the Greeks, Paul continued to preach Christ crucified. Such a Christ is "the power of God and the wisdom of God. For God's foolishness is wiser than human wisdom and God's weakness is stronger than human strength."

The gospel is about the cleansing of the temple. Jesus went up to Jerusalem, entered the temple, and cleansed it of all that took away from its holiness. On being questioned about his actions Jesus predicted that there would be a new temple, the temple of his crucified and risen body.

The truth is that we, like the Jews and the Greeks, look for Jesus in spectacular deeds and words of worldly wisdom. A true understanding of Jesus is to be found in an unlikely place – in the mystery of the cross.

1. Tell a story of looking for something and finding it in a surprising place.
2. Reflect on the Ten Commandments as basic guides in our journey to God.
3. How do you see the cross as the power and wisdom of God?
4. How does the symbolic cleansing of the temple point to Christ, the true temple, and also to us as temples of the Spirit through Christ?

Fourth Sunday of Lent

2 Chronicles 36:14-17a, 19-23
Ephesians 2:4-10
John 3:14-21

From Bad to Worse to Best

We've all found ourselves saying in a time of crisis, "And then things went from bad to worse." This expression gives us a clue to the readings for this, the fourth Sunday of Lent.

The first reading reports, "All the leading priests and the people also were exceedingly unfaithful, following all the abominations of the nations; and they polluted the house of the Lord." To remedy these abuses, God sent his messengers, "but they kept mocking the messengers of God, despising his words and scoffing at his prophets."

That was a bad state of affairs indeed. But it got even worse. "The king of the Chaldeans...burned the house of God, broke down the wall of Jerusalem, burned all its palaces...and took into exile in Babylon those who had escaped from the sword."

The Jews remained in this dire situation until a deliverer came along in the person of Cyrus the Persian. He overthrew Babylon and not only allowed the Jewish captives to return home to Jerusalem, but considered it his duty "to build him [God] a house at Jerusalem."

Thus the Jewish people of the late seventh century BCE went from bad to worse before being allowed to return home and worship in their own temple.

In the second reading Paul also describes something going from bad to worse to best. To the Ephesians he writes, "God, who is rich in mercy...even when we were dead through our trespasses, made us alive together with Christ...and raised us up with him and seated us with him in the heavenly places in Christ Jesus." Sinfulness was bad enough; when it brought about the death of Jesus, it was even worse. But then God raised him up. This was the best possible news.

In the gospel, Jesus says to Nicodemus, "Just as Moses lifted up the serpent in the wilderness, so must the Son of Man be lifted up, that whoever believes in him may have eternal life."

Soon after leaving Egypt, Moses and his people experienced much hardship in the harsh Sinai desert. They were starving and thirsty; they met up with hostile tribes and were bitten by poisonous snakes. They were saved from all these dangers.

Just so, we are saved from sin by Jesus' death and resurrection. In his own body and soul Jesus took the worst upon himself so that we might share in the best. As the gospel puts it, "For God so loved the world that he gave his only Son, so that everyone who believes in him may not perish but may have eternal life."

Indeed, as the second reading claims, "...we are what he has made us, created in Christ Jesus for good works, which God prepared beforehand to be our way of life." Our story then is truly a story of going "from bad to worse to best."

∽⊛∼

1. Describe a time in your life when things went from bad to worse to best.
2. Why is the cross, from one perspective, the worst possible news, but also the best possible news?
3. What does Paul mean when he says in verse 10 that God has created us in Christ Jesus for good works as a way of life?
4. What word or phrase from the readings will you carry with you this week?

Fifth Sunday of Lent

Jeremiah 31:31-34
Hebrews 5:7-9
John 12:20-33

Progress Has a Price Tag

A look back at human history shows that real progress has come about only at a price, often a high one. Moving from old ways to new is never easy. Many people have trouble letting go of the old ways, and those who bring in the new are often ridiculed. But without such prophetic people there could never be progress.

This also holds true in religious matters. Progress towards God comes only at the expense of leaving behind some of the old ways, some of the old visions, and accepting new ones. The readings for this fifth Sunday in Lent bear out this truth.

In the first reading, Jeremiah voices his belief in the coming of a new covenant between God and God's people. The king at that time, Josiah, was already initiating political and religious reforms. Jeremiah saw their merit and supported Josiah. In the Lord's name he proclaims, "The days are surely coming, says the Lord, when I will make a new covenant with the house of Israel and the house of Judah." It will differ from the old covenant, one written on stone, for, as the Lord says, "I will put my law within them, and I will write it on their hearts; and I will be their God, and they shall be my people."

But this new covenant did not come about as quickly as Jeremiah had hoped. Much suffering awaited the Jewish people. Their painful exile in Babylon, for instance, was but a few years away. Yet the new covenant did come eventually.

In the second reading, the author of Hebrews says, "In the days of his flesh, Jesus offered up prayers and supplications, with loud cries and tears, to the one who was able to save him from death.... Although he was a Son, he learned obedience through what he suffered; and having been made perfect, he became the source of eternal salvation for all who obey him."

The gospel makes the same point as the letter to the Hebrews. Some Greeks approach Philip asking to see the Lord. Philip, together with Andrew, passes on this request to Jesus. But Jesus gives what appears to be a strange answer. He speaks about the "hour" which has now finally come – the "hour" of the cross and of rising to new life. To explain this he speaks of the grain of wheat, which must die in order to make possible a rich harvest. What Jesus means by his answer is that to truly "see" him (as the Greeks requested), one must "see" him on the cross and in resurrection. There and there alone can one grasp him fully.

When the Church makes painful progress, and when we grow painfully in our spiritual life, we are strengthened by the knowledge that all true progress, all true growth, difficult though it may be, is new life breaking forth.

1. Describe a time in your life when you grew through a painful experience.
2. Reflect on the following words of Jeremiah from the first reading: "I will write it [the new covenant] in their hearts."
3. In the second reading, the author of Hebrews says that Jesus "learned obedience through what he suffered; and having been made perfect, he became the source of eternal salvation for all who obey him." What do these words mean to you?
4. How can we see the fullness of Jesus "on the cross and in resurrection"?

Passion Sunday

Isaiah 50:4-7
Philippians 2:6-11
Mark 14:1–15:47

Conquering Love

We are living in an increasingly secular world. The media seldom touch on matters that concern our ultimate destiny. And yet, our hearts keep searching for a message with meaning.

Deep within us is a power that heroically resists a merely materialistic view of life. See how many people sacrifice their time and money to help the needy? When a need is publicized, multitudes offer their help. So many are so generous. Thank God that this is so. The readings for Passion Sunday support and encourage the growth of a generous spirit in each of us.

In the first reading, Isaiah speaks out in the name of one to come, the suffering servant of God. "The Lord God has opened my ear, and I was not rebellious, I did not turn backward. I gave my back to those who struck me, and my cheeks to those who pulled out the beard; I did not hide my face from insult and spitting." Early Christians discovered that these words were fully realized only in Jesus.

In the second reading, Paul speaks of Jesus as one who "emptied himself, taking the form of a slave. …he humbled himself and became obedient to the point of death, even death on a cross. Therefore God highly exalted him and gave him the name that is above every name."

The gospel contains Mark's final verses in his passion narrative. He concludes with these words: "And the curtain of the temple was torn in two, from top to bottom." The centurion, who was standing at the cross, as a witness to Jesus' death, said, "Truly this man was God's Son!"

Mark thus makes clear that the old era (represented by the temple curtain) had given way to the new. Jesus, Son of God, begins a new and final era.

Take heart, then, all who struggle to love God and neighbour and in doing so meet with suffering. These, too, will receive help from God; these, too, will be "highly exalted." Right now we are in our passiontide. But victory is assured. The love of Christ overcomes the world.

1. Name a few examples you know of people helping others.
2. What especially struck you about the early Christian hymn Paul quotes in the second reading?
3. Reflect on Mark's passion account, especially on verses 38 and 39.
4. What word or phrase from the readings will you carry with you this week?

The Triduum

The "Great Sunday"

This little book offers meditations on the Sunday Lectionary readings, and well it should, for Sunday is the original Christian feast day. From the very beginnings of the faith, Christians celebrated Eucharist on the first day of the week (as reckoned according to the Jewish calendar). Why? Sunday marked for them, as it continues to do for us, the first day of the New Creation inaugurated by Christ's resurrection from the dead. By the middle of the second century, Christians began to celebrate with special solemnity the Sunday closest to the Jewish Passover, the time of year that gives the name "paschal" to the saving mystery of Christ's death and resurrection. Quite naturally, this annual Sunday celebration at Passover time was extended to include commemorations of his last supper and his crucifixion, the dramatic events of his last days. This is the origin of the Easter Triduum, the sacred days marking "the culmination of the entire liturgical year" (*General Norms for the Liturgical Year and Calendar*, § 18).

The Easter Triduum, as its name (from Latin) indicates, comprises three days as reckoned according to ancient Jewish custom—a day was measured from sundown to sundown.

Thus, the first day of the triduum commemorates his last supper (Holy Thursday evening) and his crucifixion, death, and burial (Good Friday afternoon). There are no major liturgical celebrations on the second day (from sundown on Good Friday until sundown on Holy

Saturday), for it is a period evoking the time Jesus' body rested in the tomb. The third day, the day on which Jesus rose from the dead, begins at sundown Saturday. This is the evening of the great Easter Vigil, which Saint Augustine once called the "mother of all vigils."

On these three most holy days the Church celebrates its most splendid and awe-inspiring liturgies. The Mass of the Lord's Supper on Thursday evening celebrates Jesus' last meal with his disciples when he blessed the bread and wine with the sacred words so familiar to us. This liturgy also features the ritual washing of the feet as enjoined by Jesus in John 13, and ends with the solemn procession and prayer before the reserve eucharist at a specially designated repository. The afternoon Celebration of the Lord's Passion marks the highlight of Good Friday when the Passion according to John is solemnly proclaimed, followed by special intercessory prayers for all people, the veneration of the cross, and communion. Originally celebrated from sundown on Holy Saturday evening through dawn on Easter Sunday morning, the vigil comprises the blessing of the new light and the solemn proclamation of Christ's resurrection, extensive readings from the scriptures evoking the story of salvation, the initiation of new candidates in baptism and confirmation, and culminates in the Eucharist. Easter Sunday is in essence but a continuation of this most wonderful celebration.

Anyone wishing to savour the full meaning of what each Sunday celebrates cannot miss participating in the Easter Triduum, for it is, quite simply, SUNDAY writ large.

Normand Bonneau, OMI

Easter Sunday

Acts 10:34a, 36-43
Colossians 3:1-4
John 20:1-18

Alleluia! Praise God!

After darkness comes the dawn. After trials comes success. After the pains of childbirth comes the joy of new life. Such is the story of human experience.

But never in all of history has there been a darkness like Good Friday or a joy like Easter Sunday.

The followers of Jesus gradually came to expect great things from him. Through witnessing his challenging teachings and powerful miracles, they realized that Jesus was truly the Messiah promised by God, one who would free Israel from bondage and bring in the kingdom of God.

With Jesus' death on a cross, all these expectations were thoroughly dashed. His followers ran and hid, cowering in a room behind locked doors. That was the end of the story – or it would have been, if not for Easter Sunday.

On Sunday, the first day of the week, as the first reading says, "God raised him...and allowed him to appear...to us who were chosen by God as witnesses, and who ate and drank with him after he rose from the dead."

In the second reading, Paul tells his Colossian converts that they, having been "raised with Christ," must now set their minds on the "things that are above."

In the gospel, we read how Peter and the other disciple hastened to Jesus' tomb after Mary Magdalene announced that it was empty. Peter entered the tomb first. Then the other disciple "went in, and he saw and believed."

The resurrection thus became a pivotal moment in the history of humanity. Even today we can only stand in wonder at the empty tomb and joyfully say, "Alleluia!"

1. Describe times in your life of moving from darkness to light, from sorrow to joy.
2. The followers of Jesus had no idea that it was possible for Jesus alone to rise from the dead; they knew only of the resurrection of all the dead at the end-time. In view of this, reflect on what the apostles must have thought after Jesus appeared to them.
3. What does Paul mean when he tells the Colossians that they were "raised with Christ"? How do these words apply to you and to all Christians?
4. What word or phrase from the readings will you carry with you this week?

Second Sunday of Easter

Acts 4:32-35
1 John 5:1-6
John 20:19-31

The Olympic Torch

As the date of the Olympic games draws near, torch-bearers carry a flaming torch from the site of the old games to the site of the new ones. It is a great honour for people to participate in this event, which goes back many centuries.

As privileged as these torch-bearers are, Christians have a much greater privilege. We carry the resurrection torch. We carry it not just to one place, but to all places where people live. Our message is not about a sporting event but about the assurance that through the resurrection of Jesus, God reaches out to all peoples, giving them fullness of life.

The readings for the second Sunday of the Easter season speak to us of this all-important mission, and tell us how best to carry the resurrection torch.

The first reading reminds us that if we are to be good torch-bearers, we must be closely united to one another. As Luke puts it, "The whole group of those who believed were of one heart and soul, and no one claimed private ownership of any possessions, but everything they owned was held in common."

Times have changed, of course. We are more aware of private property today. But the Christian principle hasn't changed. We must always be ready to offer our possessions, our time and our talents to those in need.

The first reading issues a challenge: "With great power the apostles gave their testimony to the resurrection of the Lord Jesus." This, too, is our challenge.

The second reading, like the first, tells us that those who bear the resurrection torch must be united and generous. "Everyone who loves the parent loves the child. By this we know that we love the children of God, when we love God and obey his commandments."

Thus it is clear that lip service is not enough for a Christian torch-bearer. The flame will be extinguished unless we truly love God above all else, do what God commands, and love our neighbours as Jesus did. The reading concludes by assuring us that we will succeed at our torch-bearing if we firmly believe that Jesus is the Son of God.

In the gospel, John tells us how the risen Jesus first appeared to his disciples and said to them, "As the Father has sent me, so I send you." When Thomas, who wasn't there when Jesus appeared, later rejoined the group and heard what had happened, he wouldn't believe. He wanted proof. So when Jesus appeared a second time he said to Thomas, "Put your finger here and see my hands.... Do not doubt but believe." Thomas responded, "My Lord and my God!" Thomas came to a deep belief, and challenges us to do the same.

Before the next Olympic Games are opened, torch-bearers will again begin the long run from the previous site to the new site. But as Christians, we always bear the resurrection torch. We must continue to hold it high for all to see. The light of Christ is needed in order that the world might live.

⌒≈❀⌒≈

1. Have you ever watched Olympic torch-bearers on TV? What do you remember about this event?
2. In the reading from Acts, Luke tells us how we must prepare ourselves to be Christian torch-bearers. Reflect on his advice.
3. Why are love of God and love of neighbour inseparable?
4. How does "doubting Thomas" help us on our faith journey?

Third Sunday of Easter

Acts 3:13-15, 17-19
1 John 2:1-5
Luke 24:35-48

The Case of the Guilty Conscience

Have you ever hurt another person in some way, then worried yourself sick about your chances of being forgiven? I think most of us have been there. We knew there was no doubt about our guilt. We were in the wrong. But would the offended party accept our apology? That was the worry.

A common experience such as the one described above can help us better appreciate the readings for this Sunday. All three of them have to do with forgiveness of sin.

In the first reading, Peter unhesitatingly confronts the leaders of the Jewish people with the crime of putting Jesus to death even though he was innocent: "But you rejected the Holy and Righteous One and asked to have a murderer given to you, and you killed the Author of life, whom God raised from the dead." Peter then softens his accusation. He says, "And now, friends, I know that you acted in ignorance, as did also your rulers.... Repent therefore, and turn to God so that your sins may be wiped out."

The second reading has a similar tone. John addresses his community in these words: "My little children, I am writing these things to you so that you may not sin. But if anyone does sin, we have an advocate with the Father, Jesus Christ the righteous; and he is the atoning sacrifice for our sins, and not for ours only but also for the sins of the whole world."

In the gospel, Jesus appears to the disciples. (This happened just after the two disciples who met him on their way to Emmaus returned to Jerusalem and told of their experience.) When Jesus appeared, the disciples were dumbfounded. They thought they were looking at a ghost! To prove that he was not a ghost, Jesus asked for food and ate with them. Then he explained to them how he had to fulfill all that was written about him in the Law of Moses, in the Prophets and in the Psalms.

Jesus continued, "Thus it is written, that the Messiah is to suffer and to rise from the dead on the third day, and that repentance and forgiveness of sins is to be proclaimed in his name to all nations, beginning from Jerusalem. You are witnesses of these things."

These readings encourage Christians to have no doubts that our sins will be forgiven. Through sinning we have offended God, and we have hurt our neighbour and ourselves, but through God's gift of love we are totally forgiven and wonderfully healed. This is "good news"! And we are its witnesses.

1. Describe a time when you had to apologize to someone for hurting them.
2. How did Jesus atone for all the sins of humanity?
3. How do you feel knowing that your sins will always be forgiven?
4. What word or phrase from the readings will you carry with you this week?

Fourth Sunday of Easter

Acts 4:7-12
1 John 3:1-2
John 10:11-18

Of Heroes and Heroines

From Greek mythology's Hercules to Superman today, we love to believe that superhuman powers are at work in the world. We look up to countless heroes and heroines as great examples of wisdom, virtue, devotion and various artistic and athletic abilities.

But all these heroes and heroines leave something to be desired. They help us, but they do not and cannot meet our deepest needs. So who can meet these needs and help us answer life's important questions?

There is only one answer: Jesus of Nazareth. He alone has been raised from the dead, transfigured in new life. His earthly words and deeds are unparalleled in human history. They strike chords in our human heart which no myth, no individual, has ever struck.

The readings for this Sunday touch on this truth.

In the first reading, from Acts, we hear Peter speaking to the rulers and elders who have questioned him about healing a cripple. He says to them, "...let it be known to all of you...that this man is standing before you in good health by the name of Jesus Christ of Nazareth, whom you crucified, whom God raised from the dead.... There is salvation in no one else, for there is no other name under heaven given among mortals by which we must be saved."

It was in the name of Jesus that Peter healed the cripple. Peter knew that this miracle was but one example of Jesus' power, that the risen Jesus is constantly working miracles in the hearts of all of us.

In the second reading, John assures us that we are indeed children of God, but that here on earth we have only a small inkling of who God is and what we will be in the next life, where we will see God "face to face" (1 Corinthians 13:12).

Jesus tells us in the gospel reading that he is indeed "the good shepherd" who loves us so much that he lays down his life for us. He knows each one of us intimately and reaches out to all who do not yet know him.

Thus Jesus, the good shepherd, is constantly with us, gradually transforming us into true daughters and sons of God. No human theory, no human power, could do this for us. Jesus can, and he does.

1. How have human heroes or heroines helped you in your struggle to live a better life?
2. How can we be "children of God"? What does that mean for us?
3. Name a particular teaching of Jesus, the good shepherd, that has helped you live a better life.
4. What word or phrase from the readings will you carry with you this week?

Fifth Sunday of Easter

Acts 9:26-31
1 John 3:18-24
John 15:1-8

Crunch Time

It is easy enough to agree to something, but harder to follow through on it. It is also easy enough to profess a belief, but harder to live up to it. But sooner or later (usually sooner), the crunch comes and we are forced to stand up, pitch in and act on our words.

Christianity is no exception. Fortunately, when the crunch comes, we have plenty of assistance, as the readings for this Sunday show.

In the first reading, Paul faces a crunch in his Christian faith. On visiting Jerusalem, Saul (Paul) was at first regarded with suspicion and fear by the Jerusalem Christians. After all, until recently, he had been persecuting them. But Barnabas took up Paul's cause, speaking of the Christian witness Paul had given in Damascus. This was just a minor crunch. Another, and a major one, arose very soon after. For "Saul went in and out among them in Jerusalem, speaking boldly in the name of the Lord." Paul spoke so boldly, the Greek-speaking Jews decided to kill him. But Paul wasn't afraid.

John starts out the second reading by stating boldly, "Little children, let us love, not in word or speech, but in truth and action." Lest anyone be disheartened by such a challenge, John quickly goes on, "Beloved, if our hearts do not condemn us, we have boldness before God; and we receive from him whatever we ask." To act out our love in real life is not easy; indeed it can be very difficult. But God is always there to encourage us.

The gospel continues the teaching of the first two readings, but in greater depth: "I am the true vine, and my Father is the vinegrower," Jesus says. "He removes every branch in me that bears no fruit. Every branch that bears fruit he prunes to make it bear more fruit." Obviously there is to be no fooling around in God's vineyard!

Jesus reassures us: "Abide in me as I abide in you.... I am the vine, you are the branches. Those who abide in me and I in them bear much fruit."

When "the crunch" comes, as it certainly will, we can meet it without fear. For Jesus is with us. His strength becomes our strength. The crunch times in our lives will bear much fruit.

1. Think about a crunch time in your life.
2. In the second reading, John says, "And this is God's commandment, that we should believe in the name of his Son Jesus Christ and love one another, just as he commanded us." Reflect on these words. How do they help us face crunch times in our faith lives?
3. The gospel tells us that Jesus is the vine and we are the branches. What does this mean to you?
4. What word or phrase from the readings will you carry with you this week?

Sixth Sunday of Easter

Acts 10:25-26, 34-35, 44-48
1 John 4:7-10
John 15:9-17

Dynamite!

In recent years we have heard much about evangelization. And that's important. For it is at the heart of our Christian faith. But what is evangelization all about?

Evangelization means a number of things, but it boils down to living out the "good news" (the gospel) and sharing it with all others. The readings for this Sunday help us do this, and do it well.

The first reading describes Peter's arrival at Caesarea (roughly 50 km/30 miles north of Jaffa [Tel Aviv]). He is met by Cornelius, who is a pagan, and a centurion of the Roman cohort that is stationed there. Cornelius falls at Peter's feet in worship. Peter says, "Stand up; I am only a mortal." Then Peter says to all present, "I truly understand that God shows no partiality, but in every nation anyone who fears him and does what is right is acceptable to him." (Remember Peter's vision in Jaffa of the sheet containing unclean food, which he was commanded to eat. At first Peter refused because it was unclean. Then God cleansed it. This was the beginning of Peter's understanding that God could make pagans "clean.")

While Peter is still speaking, the Holy Spirit comes down upon the listeners, causing them to proclaim God's greatness in various languages. Following this manifestation Peter orders them to be baptized.

In the second reading, John encourages his people to love one another for, as he says, "...everyone who loves is born of God and knows God." Notice that John draws no definite line here between believer and unbeliever. *Everyone* who loves is of God; as the well-known antiphon puts it, "Where love is, there is God."

The gospel deepens our understanding of love. Jesus says, "As the Father has loved me, so I have loved you; abide in my love. If you keep my commandments, you will remain in my love." In case we miss the point of these words, Jesus adds, "This is my commandment, that you love one another as I have loved you." Loving God and our neighbour is thus the very basis of evangelization.

Jesus makes it clear that we have been called: "You did not choose me but I chose you. And I appointed you to go and bear fruit, fruit that will last."

To sum up, evangelization means enabling the good news of the gospel to sink into every fibre of our being, a process that continues for our whole lives. At the same time, it means going out and "bearing fruit." In loving concern we go out to others so that they, too, will benefit from this good news.

Evangelization is dynamite! – an explosive force that is meant to disrupt evil and transform human lives. And we are the ones chosen to light the fuse.

1. Give examples of good news that you have heard or told to others, such as the end of a war, the birth of a baby, or a young couple's engagement.
2. Reflect on Peter's first experience of taking the gospel (the good news) to pagans.
3. In the second reading, we learn that where love is, there is God. How does this truth help us evangelize?
4. How is each Christian commissioned by Jesus to share the good news with others?

Ascension of the Lord

Acts 1:1-11
Ephesians 4:1-13
Mark 16:15-20

Preparing for the Mission

We all know what it is to be prepared for a task. Years of schooling and practical experience help us to live in the fast-moving world of today. Some people go on to college or university to train and study for specialized tasks. Even once we have started on the task, we may need further preparation before advancing to higher positions.

In the same way, Jesus prepared his followers for carrying out the greatest of all tasks: witnessing to Jesus and his teachings. On this feast of the Ascension, we read of the final preparation Jesus gives to his disciples.

In the first reading, from Acts, Luke tells us that Jesus, after his resurrection, spent a final forty days with the apostles, "speaking [to them] about the kingdom of God." Just as he had spent forty days preparing for his public ministry, he now takes forty days giving final instructions for the Church's public ministry.

At the end of the forty days, Jesus says to the apostles, "...you will receive power when the Holy Spirit has come upon you; and you will be my witnesses in Jerusalem, in all Judea and Samaria, and to the ends of the earth." After this promise Jesus "was lifted up, and a cloud took him out of their sight."

To help the apostles understand that spreading the gospel was now up to them, "...two men in white robes stood by them. They said, 'Men of Galilee, why do you stand looking up toward heaven? This Jesus, who has been taken from you into heaven, will come in the same way as you saw him go into heaven.'"

In the second reading, Paul tells the Ephesians, and all Christians, how to proceed in the Christian mission: "with all humility and gentleness, with patience, bearing with one another in love, making every effort to maintain the unity of the Spirit in the bond of peace." He also points out to them, and to us, that there are different gifts in the mission. Some will be prophets, others evangelists, others will be pastors and teachers. All these gifts are "for building up the body of Christ."

In the gospel, Jesus commissions the eleven: "Go into all the world and proclaim the good news to the whole creation." After Jesus was taken up, the eleven "went out and proclaimed the good news everywhere...."

As the Lord worked with them, so he works with us. We, too, have the immense privilege of announcing and helping to build God's kingdom in the world today.

~⊛~

1. What training have you had for the work you do? How did this training prepare you for your work?
2. How did Jesus prepare his followers for the mission he gave them?
3. We are all called to be evangelists, bearers of the "good news." How do you see yourself carrying out this mission? (Remember St. Theresa, the Little Flower. Though she spent her short life in a cloister, she became the patron of missionaries.)
4. What word or phrase from the readings will you carry with you this week?

Pentecost

Acts 2:1-11
Galatians 5:16-25
John 15:26-27; 16:12-15

That's the Spirit!

We often hear the above expression – in praise of someone who tackles a job or a problem with great gusto, or in praise of a sports team or any group of people doing a particular task. If an individual or a team has "spirit," there is a greater chance of succeeding. Even teams with expert participants fail if they lack "spirit." This intangible thing called "spirit" is present in so many human activities. But one spirit stands above all others: the "Holy Spirit."

In the beginning, this Spirit hovered over the waters of chaos, bringing order. It worked among the people of the Old Testament, bringing them peace, vision and direction. But this Spirit was simply another name for God, and was not distinguished as a person.

In the New Testament, Jesus promised that this same Spirit would be with his followers. On Pentecost Sunday we celebrate the powerful manifestation of the Spirit to the first Christians, and also realize that the Spirit is a distinct person within the Trinity.

In the first reading, from Acts, Luke tells us how "divided tongues, as of fire," appeared among the gathered Christians. They were "filled with the Holy Spirit and began to speak in other languages." The people in the crowd, who were from various cultures in the Mediterranean area, each heard the apostles speak in their own native tongue. Out of the babble of noise came order.

In the second reading, Paul tells his Galatian converts to "live by the Spirit." They must turn away from "the works of the flesh" (fornication, impurity, licentiousness, idolatry, sorcery, enmities, strife, etc.) and aim instead for the "fruit of the Spirit" (love, joy, patience, kindness, generosity, etc.). He says to them: "If we live by the Spirit, let us also be guided by the Spirit."

In the gospel, Jesus promises his followers that when the Spirit comes, "...he will guide you into all the truth.... He will glorify me, because he will take what is mine and declare it to you."

The same Holy Spirit continues to be with us today: within us, bringing peace and joy in hectic times, and with the whole Church, guiding it through the turmoil of a broken world. The Spirit will never leave us – never. With the Spirit, we will triumph.

1. Describe a person or group of people you have met who had an indomitable spirit, who never gave up hope.
2. What do you think happened to the first Christians on Pentecost Sunday?
3. Paul told the Galatians, "If we live by the Spirit, let us also be guided by the Spirit." What do these words mean?
4. Do you find comfort in Jesus' promise that the Spirit will "guide us into all truth"? Why?

Trinity Sunday

Deuteronomy 4:32-34, 39-40
Romans 8:14-17
Matthew 28:16-20

Interpersonal Relations

Despite advances in the social and psychological sciences, we still have trouble relating to one another at times. Many of our friendships are superficial. Marital breakdowns are becoming the rule rather than the exception.

Why is this the case? Why do we not relate to others in a more meaningful way? Perhaps it's due to the kind of world we live in: a world where business comes first, where so many scramble to make a living and have little time for fostering deep relationships.

Whatever the cause, there is a remedy. We find it, at least implicitly, in the readings for this Trinity Sunday. Why implicitly? Because the three readings point directly to our relationship with God.

The first reading, from the Book of Deuteronomy, gives us the basic rules for fostering a right relationship with God our creator: we must "keep his statutes and his commandments." Doing so guarantees "your own well-being and that of your descendants after you," as the reading says.

In the second reading, Paul makes clear that we are "children of God." As such we can cry, "Abba! Father!" He adds that we are "heirs of God and joint heirs with Christ."

In the gospel, Jesus, in very clear terms, commissions us thus: "All authority in heaven and on earth has been given to me. Go therefore and make disciples of all nations, baptizing them in the name of the Father and of the Son and of the Holy Spirit."

How do these three readings help us deepen our relationships with one another? Because, through baptism, we are all children of the triune God. This makes us faith brothers and sisters; we are a faith family bonded by trinitarian love.

But although our baptismal heritage makes us brothers and sisters, we must strive constantly to come to a deeper love and respect for one another. This includes those who are not baptized, for we are sent to them also. They, too, are made in God's image.

Every human being has immense potential. To help others explore and develop this potential is our great challenge. May we pursue it diligently, with love and humility.

1. What are some of your struggles with interpersonal relationships? Give a few examples.
2. Reflect on the teaching of the first reading, which tells us how we are to relate to God.
3. How does the second reading deepen our relationship with God?
4. In baptism we are immersed in the Trinity. How does this immersion help us in our interpersonal relationships?

Body and Blood of Christ

Exodus 24:3-8
Hebrews 9:11-15
Mark 14:12-16, 22-26

Life's Deep Mysteries

It is easy to talk about the ordinary moments and details of life – the funny things, the good things and the not-so-good things. Talking about life itself, its inner meaning, is much more difficult.

It is much the same with our faith. We find it easy to speak about what Jesus said and did, but we stumble when it comes time to speak of the mysteries of Jesus' life. Yet we must try to speak of them, for through these mysteries we discover our Christian identity.

This Sunday we celebrate the feast of the Body and Blood of Christ (Corpus Christi), a feast that touches on the basic mystery of our redemption and thus helps us explore and speak of this great mystery.

The first reading begins this way: "Moses came and told the people all the words of the Lord and all the ordinances; and all the people answered with one voice, and said, 'All the words that the Lord has spoken we will do.'" To seal this covenant between God and his people, Moses had an altar built and directed that the blood of animal sacrifice be offered upon it. Then Moses "took the blood and dashed it on the people, and said, 'See the blood of the covenant that the Lord has made with you in accordance with all these words.'" To ancient peoples, blood was the symbol of life. It was therefore a most fitting symbol for the covenant God made with his people.

In the second reading, we discover how much Jesus furthers this covenant relationship with God. "Christ came as a high priest of the good things that have come.... He entered once for all into the Holy Place, not with the blood of goats and calves, but with his own blood, thus obtaining eternal redemption." The author of the reading then concludes, "Christ is the mediator of a new covenant...because a death has occurred that redeems them from the transgressions under the first covenant." The new covenant is thus far superior to the old.

The gospel reveals what Christ did at the feast of Unleavened Bread, the Paschal Feast. "While they were eating, Jesus took a loaf of bread, and after blessing it he broke it, gave it to them and said, 'Take; this is my body.'" After taking the cup, all drank from it. Then Jesus said, "This is my blood of the covenant, which is poured out for many."

Here we are at the heart of the new covenant, at the heart of Christ's love for us. He gives himself totally to his Father and to us. He challenges us to do the same. When we eat and drink the bread and wine of the Eucharist, we are saying "yes" to Jesus just as our faith ancestors said "yes" to Moses. They promised to obey the old covenant law. We, however, promise to love God and neighbour above all else, as Jesus did. This is the new covenant.

The mystery of the Eucharist is to be lived out through loving God and one another. Celebrating the Eucharist empowers us to keep living out this mystery in our daily lives, and living it ever more deeply. By doing so we are assured that just as God raised Jesus from the dead into eternal life, God will do the same for us.

1. Our lives are filled with such mysteries as birth, suffering, love, death. How can we begin to understand these mysteries?
2. Reflect on Moses' fashioning of the old covenant, described in the first reading.
3. Why, according to the second reading, is the new covenant superior to the old?
4. In light of the truth that we are all true celebrants, what does celebrating the Eucharist mean to you?

Tenth Sunday in Ordinary Time

Genesis 3:8-15
2 Corinthians 4:13–5:1
Mark 3:20-35

Passing the Buck

Since the beginning of time, humans have loved to "pass the buck." Most of us are good at ducking responsibility. We'd rather others take it. This Sunday's readings explore this very human tendency.

In the first reading, Adam blames Eve when God asks him about eating the forbidden fruit. Eve, in turn, blames the serpent. This bad start in our human enterprise could have been disastrous. Instead, God declared to the serpent that the Messiah to come would strike his head, whereas all the serpent could do was strike at the Messiah's heel.

The second reading backs up God's promise to Adam and Eve. Paul tells the Corinthians, and us, not to lose heart in the midst of life's many afflictions. He concludes, "For we know that if the earthly tent we live in is destroyed, we have a building from God, a house not made with hands, eternal in the heavens."

The gospel begins by noting that people were saying of Jesus, "He has gone out of his mind." They were passing the buck. They couldn't accept his teaching – it was just too true!

Even the scribes (lawyers) from Jerusalem were not above buck-passing. They wouldn't admit that Jesus could cast out demons on his own authority. They said he did so by the power of Beelzebub, the ruler of demons.

But the gospel ends on an encouraging note. After hearing that his family wanted to speak to him, Jesus said, "Who are my mother and my brothers?" Then, looking at those around him, he said, "Here are my mother and my brothers!"

Our real strength is thus in our union in faith with Jesus. In him, and him alone, we'll have the strength to take responsibility and avoid passing the buck.

1. Talk about times when you (or someone you know) passed the buck.
2. Reflect on Adam and Eve's effort to avoid taking responsibility.
3. Reflect on Paul's advice to the Thessalonians (last paragraph).
4. How do you feel when you hear Jesus say that we are part of his family?

Eleventh Sunday in Ordinary Time

Ezekiel 17:22-24
2 Corinthians 5:6-10
Mark 4:26-34

Our Dreams Come and Go – God's Do Not

How often have you dreamed of making a fortune; rescuing a loved one; attaining great success in sport, in science, in politics or on the stage?

How often have your dreams come true? And even when they did, were you completely satisfied? Or did you keep dreaming new dreams?

Such are human dreams – they fade and die. God's dreams are different: God's dreams come true. The three readings for this Sunday follow the unfolding of God's dream for us – a dream called "the kingdom of God."

In the first reading, Ezekiel gives flesh to God's dream of a kingdom in these words: "Thus says the Lord God: 'I myself will take a sprig from the lofty top of a cedar.... I myself will plant it on a high and lofty mountain...in order that it may produce boughs and bear fruit, and become a noble cedar.'" This "noble cedar" is God's kingdom.

In the second reading, Paul notes that "we are always confident, even though we know that while we are at home in the body we are away from the Lord – for we walk by faith, not by sight." All the while, the kingdom is alive and growing.

In the gospel, Jesus explains God's kingdom more fully. To the crowds he says, "The kingdom of God is as if someone would scatter seed on the ground, and would sleep and rise night and day, and the seed would sprout and grow, without the sower knowing how…. But when the grain is ripe, at once he goes in with the sickle, because the harvest has come."

Jesus goes on to tell a second parable about the kingdom. It "is like a mustard seed, which, when sown upon the ground, is the smallest of all the seeds on earth; yet when it is sown it grows up and becomes the greatest of all shrubs, and puts forth large branches, so that the birds of the air can make nests in its shade."

This, then, is God's dream for us, God's supreme gift to humanity. It comes to us through the redeeming Son and sanctifying Spirit.

This kingdom of God, God's dream for us, is still unfolding. It is invisible so we find it hard to grasp. It doesn't make national headlines, yet it is in our midst, growing in the soil of human hearts. At the end-time, however, it will be emblazoned in the heavens, clear and unmistakable. For God will then be "all in all." And we, God's children, will reap the many blessings of the dream – eternally.

1. Have any of your dreams gone astray? How does this make you feel?
2. What does the reading from Ezekiel tell us about God's kingdom?
3. How do Paul's thoughts in the second reading fit into the picture of God's kingdom?
4. Reflect on the two gospel parables about the kingdom. How is the kingdom like a seed that is sown?

Twelfth Sunday in Ordinary Time

Job 38:1-4, 8-11
2 Corinthians 5:14-17
Mark 4:35-41

Trust Is Part of Life

How can we as individuals know that the food we eat or the product we use will live up to the claims that have been made about it? We have neither the time nor the expertise to do the necessary testing, so we trust in the testing done by government and other agencies. Otherwise we'd be afraid to eat the food we buy or to use modern technology.

And what about our friends? Do we trust them? If we do not trust them but insist on continual proof of their friendship, we will surely lose them.

Trust is also indispensable in our relationship with God. For if, instead of trusting, we insist on proof of his loving care, if we demand miracles as the price of our continuing relationship with God, watch out! We'll end up in deep trouble. This Sunday's readings make it clear that God can be trusted.

The first reading is from the book of Job. Job had a big question to ask God. He wanted to know why he had to suffer so much. In those days, suffering was thought to be a punishment for sin. Job knew he was living a good life; why, then, did God send so many calamities his way?

Towards the end of the book, Job receives his answer. It wasn't at all what he expected. From the heart of a tempest God spoke to him. He reminded Job how little he, and all humans, really know. For instance, he asked Job, "Who shut in the sea with doors when it burst out from the womb?" Of course Job knew that God had done so, but Job didn't have a clue how God did it. If God acted so wisely and power-fully, surely Job ought to trust God.

In the second reading, Paul reminds the Corinthians of the great love Christ has for them. Because of such generous love, "there is new creation: everything old has passed away; see, everything has become new!" We trust in this newness.

The gospel describes the disciples rowing with Jesus across the Sea of Galilee. Suddenly a storm came up. Jesus was asleep. The disciples said to him, "'Teacher, do you not care that we are perishing?' He woke up, rebuked the wind, and said to the sea, 'Peace! Be still!' Then the wind ceased, and there was a dead calm."

The lesson in these three readings is crystal clear: trust in God. We may not be able to answer all life's questions, or solve all life's problems, but we can know this: no storm, no calamity, nothing whatsoever will thwart God's loving plan for those who trust in him.

1. When has your trust in human "experts" or agencies paid off? When has that trust been broken in your life?

2. Reflect on God's answer to Job at the end of the first reading.

3. In Christ, Paul assures us in the second reading, "everything has been made new." What does this mean to you?

4. How does the gospel apply to the stormy times we experience in our lives?

Thirteenth Sunday in Ordinary Time

Wisdom 1:13-15; 2:23-24
2 Corinthians 8:7, 9, 13-15
Mark 5:21-43

What Seems to Be a Tragedy Isn't Always So

Seed is sown. It dies in the soil. But in dying it gives rise to new life. Leaves fall and decay. But in doing so they nourish the growth of new life. When winter comes, growth stops. But spring brings a renewal. Nature's cycle teaches us that what at first appears tragic is not always so. Out of death comes life.

This Sunday's readings assure us that this cycle also exists in human life.

The first reading, from the book of Wisdom, begins by making clear God's attitude towards death. Death is not God's doing. God "does not delight in the death of the living."

The author continues: "For God created us for incorruption, and made us in the image of his own eternity, but through the devil's envy death entered the world, and those who belong to his company experience it." Our immortality was linked to our relationships with God. The devil knew this and tempted humans to break with God. He succeeded, but not as fully as he thought.

In the gospel, Jesus is approached by Jairus, a synagogue official, who begs him to come and heal his sick daughter. Jesus starts out towards Jairus' house, but before Jesus gets there, "some people came from the leader's house to say, 'Your daughter is dead. Why trouble the teacher any further?'"

Jesus, however, says to the official, "Do not fear, only believe." Coming into the man's home, Jesus takes the dead child's hand and says, "Little girl, get up!" The girl immediately gets up.

Jesus overcame death. He restored life to the official's daughter. But the meaning of the miracle is much deeper. He restored physical life to only three people: the little girl in today's reading, the son of the widow of Nain, and Lazarus. But to every individual of the human race Jesus offers restoration to life in God. This is a far greater miracle – and we all share in it.

The second reading, where Paul encourages the Corinthians to be generous to others, at first seems to have little reference to restoration of life, but this very generosity comes from the life which Jesus gives us. As Paul says, "though he was rich, yet for your sakes he became poor, so that by his poverty you might become rich." The life to which Jesus restores us thus enables us to help others in their need.

Death, then, is never what God wants. Richness of life is God's desire. Yet true richness of life springs from a willingness to give, to empty ourselves. It is only when we die to ourself that we make room for new life.

1. Name some other examples of dying/rising, or offer deeper insights into the examples given.
2. Through sinfulness, we humans thwarted God's plan for us. Reflect on this mystery of evil.
3. Reflect on Jesus' raising of the little girl from the dead.
4. Paul tells the Corinthians that our spiritual poverty can enrich others. What does this mean to you?

Fourteenth Sunday in Ordinary Time

Ezekiel 2:2-5
2 Corinthians 12:7-10
Mark 6:1-6

Whistling in the Wind

Have you ever sounded a cautionary note in the midst of an enthusiastic meeting or uttered sombre advice while people were making merry? Have you ever mentioned the possibility of defeat to people dreaming of victory, or mentioned a doubt when all present were sure they had the right answer?

How hard it is to go against the grain! Yet that's exactly what prophets were called upon to do. This was a sure recipe for being unpopular.

If we tend to ignore prophecy, or if we are shirking our own prophetic calling, it will help to reflect on this Sunday's readings.

In the first reading, Ezekiel discovers the difficulties of being a prophet. Near the start of the Babylonian exile, his compatriots raise their voices in bitter complaint and anger at their fate. It wasn't a propitious time to speak out for God, yet, as Ezekiel explains, "...a spirit entered into me and set me on my feet; and I heard him speaking to me."

What the spirit said was this: "Mortal, I am sending you to the people of Israel, to a nation of rebels who have rebelled against me.... Whether they hear or refuse to hear...they shall know there has been a prophet among them."

The life of a prophet is not a bed of roses. They usually do not see immediate results. Much of the time, they seem to be whistling in the wind.

And yet, as Paul discovered, it is in weakness that prophets find their strength. In the second reading, Paul complains to God about a thorn in the flesh that was prohibiting him, as he thought, from effectively proclaiming God's word. Three times he asked God to be rid of it. But God replied, "My grace is sufficient for you; for power is made perfect in weakness."

In the gospel, Jesus himself feels inadequate as he faces an angry hometown audience. When he spoke to them they said, "'Where did this man get all this?'... And they took offense at him. And Jesus could do no deed of power there."

We all take part in prophesying. We are asked to listen to prophets and we are challenged to speak out prophetically in the name of Christ. Both of these duties will often prove difficult and discouraging. At these times we will do well to remember Paul's words in today's second reading: "for whenever I am weak, then I am strong."

1. Describe a time when you spoke out against something that others approved of. How did you feel? Why did you take the stand you did?
2. Ezekiel had his marching orders from God. He had to speak out, no matter what the result! Reflect on this insight into prophecy.
3. How is "power made perfect in weakness," as God made clear to Paul?
4. Why are prophets not usually accepted in their own time and place?

Fifteenth Sunday in Ordinary Time

Amos 7:12-15
Ephesians 1:3-14
Mark 6:7-13

Prophets in Tough Times

An old proverb assures us that "a word to the wise is sufficient." Unfortunately, however, not everyone is wise – some are immature, unthinking, foolish, and even downright evil. How do Christians, prophets as we are, prepare ourselves to face these kinds of people? The readings for this Sunday come to our aid.

The first reading tells us about Amaziah, a priest in Bethel (a famous shrine in Northern Israel), curtly sending the prophet Amos back to southern Israel. But Amos didn't take Amaziah's dismissal lying down. He told Amaziah that he himself was not a so-called professional prophet (these were usually hired by the king, and often told him what he wanted to hear), but that God himself took Amos from his job of tending sycamore trees and commissioned him to prophesy in the rich land of northern Israel. And prophesy Amos did, in plain, bold terms.

In the second reading, Paul tells the Ephesians, and us, that we are chosen "in Christ" to be witnesses to the world of God's plan – "to gather up all things in Christ, things in heavens and things on earth" – which will come about in the fullness of time. What a wonderful challenge lies ahead of us!

In the gospel, Jesus authorizes the twelve apostles to cure "unclean spirits" (that is, to face and overcome evil) and to call people to repentance.

As Christians, therefore, and as prophets, we, too, are authorized by Jesus to face and overcome evil in the world, and to call people to change their lives in view of God's plan in Christ: to bring humanity and the universe to final fulfillment. Our path, like the paths of all the prophets, will not be easy. But the news we witness to is the greatest news the world has ever heard and, in the end, God's plan will succeed.

1. Describe a time when you had to give a message to people who were not very open to what you had to say.
2. Amos set out to warn the rich people of northern Israel that their conduct went against God's will. What do you think Amos' message would be to the world of today?
3. In the second reading, Paul outlines God's plan for humanity and the universe. Reflect on this plan. What does it mean for our world now?
4. We, like the apostles, are authorized to spread the good news, overcome evil and call others to change their lives. How do you feel about this challenge?

Sixteenth Sunday in Ordinary Time

Jeremiah 23:1-6
Ephesians 2:13-18
Mark 6:30-34

Self-serving

There's nothing wrong with serving oneself at gas stations, laundromats or cafeterias, but there's something terribly wrong with self-serving people, especially people in leadership positions. Self-serving people look for their own good first and let others have the leftovers. Although we might hate to admit it, there's something of this spirit in all of us. So all of us can learn from this Sunday's readings.

In the first reading, the prophet Jeremiah knows that the current king, Zedekiah, is selfish and inept. Indeed, his actions brought about the fall of Jerusalem. So Jeremiah, in God's name, cries out, "Woe to the shepherds who destroy and scatter the sheep of my pasture!"

But Jeremiah sees better days ahead. "The days are surely coming...when I will raise up for David a righteous Branch, and he shall reign as king and deal wisely, and shall execute justice and righteousness in the land."

In the second reading, Paul sees that Jesus fulfilled Jeremiah's prophecy far beyond Jeremiah's wildest imaginings. For Jesus, the true shepherd, reached out not only to the people of Israel, but to all humanity. As Paul puts it, Jesus "abolished the law with its commandments and ordinances, that he might create in himself one new humanity."

In the gospel, Jesus invites his followers to "come away to a deserted place all by yourselves and rest a while." Their rest was short-lived; crowds of people guessed where they were going and got there first. What does Jesus do? Shoo them away? No: "he had compassion for them, because they were like sheep without a shepherd; and he began to teach them many things."

For Jesus, people come first. In teaching the crowds on a day when he might have preferred to rest, he taught his followers to put others ahead of themselves.

1. Spend a few moments in silence, looking for evidence of self-seeking in your own life.
2. Some people in Jesus' day put all their faith in the Law, believing that it alone made them righteous. Jeremiah foretells that "The Lord is our righteousness." Reflect on this prophecy of Jeremiah's.
3. In the second reading, Paul tells us that Jesus created in himself "a new humanity." What does this mean?
4. Reflect on the lesson Jesus teaches us in the gospel.

Seventeenth Sunday in Ordinary Time

2 Kings 4:42-44
Ephesians 4:1-6
John 6:1-15

Missing the Point

How good we are at missing the point! We are often so preoccupied with our own agenda, our own little world, that when someone tries to widen our horizon or deepen our views, we simply miss the point.

Parents are very aware of this scenario. As they strive to share some of life's deeper meanings with their children, their words often fall on deaf ears, especially if those ears belong to teenagers. Teenagers are usually caught up in the present moment, in the now. Words of deeper wisdom can take a long time to sink in!

God is no doubt also very aware of this scenario. We often miss the point God is making. Fortunately, God doesn't give up until we've caught at least a glimmer of his teaching, as we discover in this Sunday's readings.

The first reading, from the second book of Kings, and the gospel are both about feeding a large group of people with a pitifully small amount of food.

When Elisha, in the first reading, told the man who brought him food to "give it to the people and let them eat," the man answered, "How can I set this before a hundred people?" The same thing happens in the gospel. When Jesus suggests that the disciples feed a large group, Philip replies, "Six months' wages would not buy enough bread." Simon Peter's brother, Andrew, says, "There is a boy here who has five barley loaves and two fish. But what are they among so many people?"

In both readings, a miracle takes place and all are fed. But both groups miss the real point. God wasn't out just to fill people's bellies, but to satisfy their spiritual hunger. The miracle merely points to that truth. The crowd with Jesus missed the point: the people wanted to make him king so that they would have an unending supply of bread.

In the second reading, Paul tries to stretch the faith horizon of his Ephesian converts by reminding them, and us, that God the Father "is above all and through all and in all." In other words, Paul tells us that God is present in all reality. There is no event, no occasion, no place wherein God is absent. On the contrary, God is actively present everywhere. Hence we must continually stretch the limits of our mind and heart to grasp the meaning of such presence.

1. When have you missed the point of a reading, an event or someone's words?
2. John calls Jesus' miracles "signs." Can you think why he uses that term? What are the miracles signs of?
3. The gospels are full of miracles (or signs). Do we need miracles today? Why or why not?
4. What word or phrase from the readings will you carry with you this week?

Eighteenth Sunday in Ordinary Time

Exodus 16:2-4, 12-15, 31a
Ephesians 4:17, 20-24
John 6:24-35

More Than You Ever Expected!

Have you ever been pleasantly surprised by receiving more than you asked for or expected? Perhaps it was your birthday or Christmas. Perhaps you took a trip and enjoyed it more than you thought you would. Or perhaps you had a meal that turned out to be a delectable banquet. Life is full of surprises.

The Bible, too, is filled with surprising stories. This Sunday's readings include two of them.

The first reading describes how the Israelites, newly freed from Egypt, were having a hard time finding food in the desert. They started to complain, then lo and behold! Flocks of quail, weak from crossing the Mediterranean, flopped all around them. All they had to do was pick them up. In addition, each morning they were able to gather up manna, a fine white substance from a desert plant. It tasted good and was plentiful.

In the gospel, Jesus says to the crowd for whom he had multiplied bread and fish: "You are looking for me, not because you saw signs, but because you ate your fill of the loaves." He reminds them that their ancestors were given manna to eat while they journeyed in the wilderness.

Then Jesus says to them, "This is the work of God, that you believe in him whom he has sent." Jesus continues: "Very truly, I tell you, it was not Moses who gave you the bread from heaven, but it is my

Father who gives you the true bread from heaven." He tells them: "I am the bread of life."

Talk about receiving more than we expected! Whoever would have thought that in and through the Son, God would become our very food, food "that gives life to the world."

In the second reading, Paul touches upon the same kind of surprise when he tells the Ephesians that they are "to be renewed in the spirit of your minds, and to clothe yourselves with the new self, created according to the likeness of God in true righteousness and holiness." This is God's gift of self to us.

1. Talk about some of the good surprises you have had in your life.
2. Picture yourself in a hostile desert land with little to eat. Suddenly you have a supply of fresh meat and a sweet substance called manna to eat. How do you feel?
3. What does it mean to you to partake of the body and blood of Christ in the Eucharist?
4. What word or phrase from the readings will you carry with you this week?

Nineteenth Sunday in Ordinary Time

1 Kings 19:4-8
Ephesians 4:30–5:2
John 6:41-51

Food for Pilgrims

In ancient times, long journeys were few and far between – mainly because transportation was slow. But times have changed. Now we can go long distances in a short time and with all the comforts of home.

There is one journey, however, that has always remained much the same – our journey, our pilgrimage to fullness of life in God. This is the most important journey of our lives, since it has to do with our ultimate destiny. The readings for this Sunday have much to say about this pilgrimage.

In the first reading, we find the prophet Elijah fleeing for his life from Queen Jezebel, who was angry at him for besting her false prophets. He left Mount Carmel, in northern Israel, and headed for Mount Sinai (also called Mount Horeb), in the far south. After only a day's journey, he was ready to give up and forfeit his life. But an angel came to him with food to strengthen him, not once but twice, and Elijah was finally able to reach the safety of Mount Sinai.

In the second reading, Paul advises his Ephesian converts on how best to continue their Christian pilgrimage: "put away from you all bitterness...and be kind to one another"; "be imitators of God...and live in love, as Christ loved us."

The gospel is a continuation from last Sunday, wherein Jesus spoke about the bread from heaven that gives life to the world. In today's gospel, Jesus enlarges upon the same theme. Because he himself is living bread come down from heaven, he promises that "Whoever eats of this bread will live forever; and the bread that I will give is my flesh for the life of the world."

What wonderful food we have for our journey to God! It is the best food we could have, and it guarantees that we will reach our destination: full participation in the very life of God. How could we ask for more?

1. Elijah was the first true prophet in the history of Israel. Why was Jezebel so angry with him?
2. How does the second reading help us on our pilgrimage to God?
3. How is Jesus "living bread" in the Eucharist? Reflect on his words in the gospel.
4. What word or phrase from the readings will you carry with you this week?

Twentieth Sunday in Ordinary Time

Proverbs 9:1-6
Ephesians 5:15-20
John 6:51-58

Come to the Banquet

It is always nice to be invited to a feast – a wedding reception, a dinner to honour someone, a special occasion. The readings for this Sunday are full of images of food and drink – images of feasting.

In the part of the book of Proverbs from which the first reading is taken, Wisdom and Folly both invite the "simple" to their banquet. Verses 1 to 6 of chapter 9 contain Wisdom's invitation. They tell us that "Wisdom has built her house" and "set her table." She invites the simple-hearted to "come, eat of my bread and drink of the wine I have mixed." Thus are we invited to feast on true wisdom.

In the second reading, Paul's words to the Ephesians echo Wisdom's invitation. He tells the Ephesians, and us, to live "not as unwise people but as wise"; he then advises, "So do not be foolish, but understand what the will of the Lord is."

The gospel continues the theme of the two previous Sundays, namely, that Jesus himself is "the living bread that came down from heaven. Whoever eats of this bread will live forever."

The eucharistic banquet is thus the greatest feast of all. We are fed with the word of God in the readings, and we receive the life of the resurrected Christ in the Eucharist. Through Christ we are taken up into the life of God.

How can we even think of refusing God's invitation to come to the banquet?

1. How does the first reading offer a foretaste of the Eucharist?
2. How do Paul's words in the second reading relate to the theme of the Eucharist?
3. How does Jesus come to us in the celebration of the Eucharist?
4. What word or phrase from the readings will you carry with you this week?

Twenty-first Sunday in Ordinary Time

Joshua 24:1-2a, 15-17, 18b
Ephesians 4:32–5:2, 21-32
John 6:53, 60-69

Loyalty

It is not easy to be loyal when we are faced with difficult choices. If a cause we support turns out to go against something we believe in, what should we do? If friends divorce, where should our loyalties lie?

Loyalty crops up in the readings for this Sunday.

In the first reading, Joshua gathers the tribes of Israel at Shechem (an ancient shrine from the time of Abraham, about 50 km/30 miles north of Jerusalem). There Joshua challenges the tribes' loyalty to God. The people reply that they "will serve the Lord, for he is our God."

In the second reading, Paul advises his Ephesian converts on how to relate to one another. He encourages them to have a "tenderhearted, forgiving" relationship, one in which all are to be "subject to one another." At that time, in the Greco-Roman world, certain accepted moral and household codes existed. Paul respects these codes. Today we have a more mature understanding of spousal relationships, and may find it hard to accept Paul's words. And yet, all the qualities Paul mentions could be summed up in the expression "loyal love."

The gospel continues the eucharistic theme of the past two Sundays (taken from the sixth chapter of John). Jesus issues a challenge to his followers: "…unless you eat the flesh of the Son of Man and drink his blood, you have no life in you." In those days, "flesh and blood" stood for the whole person, body and soul.

In receiving the Eucharist we are receiving Jesus (in his resurrected life). The Eucharist is for real. Through the Eucharist, Jesus offers himself to us in an intimate and holy union. This union demands our loyalty – are we able to offer it?

∽⊛∾

1. Describe an experience of being loyal or of someone showing loyalty to you.
2. Imagine yourself among the people of Joshua's day (somewhere around the thirteenth century BCE). How would you answer his challenge to be true to God even though it meant entering and conquering the land of Israel?
3. Reflect on Paul's advice to the Ephesians, particularly on the spousal relationship and how it is a symbol of Christ's relationship to the Church.
4. Why is the Eucharist Christ's greatest challenge to us?

Twenty-second Sunday
in Ordinary Time

Deuteronomy 4:1-2, 6-8
James 1:17-18, 21-22, 27
Mark 7:1-8, 14-15, 21-23

Laws Need a Vision

In my high school days I was much taken with the following phrase from Richard Lovelace's poem "To Lacusta": "I could not love thee dear so much, loved I not honour more." The gentleman lover of Lacusta was called to take up arms in defence of his country. Were he to refuse he would be less a man, and so, less a husband to Lacusta.

Such a truth enables us to understand the teachings in this Sunday's readings.

In the first reading, the author of Deuteronomy urges his readers to recognize that the laws and ordinances of Moses came from God and mirror God's wisdom. Notice how the author goes out of his way to make clear that the God who gave us his laws is very near to us. God hears us "whenever we call to him."

In the second reading, James teaches us that God "gave us birth by the word of truth." He goes on to say that it isn't enough to hear the word; we must act on it. We are "to care for orphans and widows in their distress, and to keep [ourselves] unstained by the world."

The gospel makes it clear that human laws and customs are time-conditioned. They serve a good purpose, but when new facts are discovered or a deeper understanding is acquired, laws need to change.

With the coming of Jesus, something wonderfully new happened. He came to bring Israel to its fulfillment.

To do so, he gave God's people a new vision of life, one that had to do with the very depths of the human heart.

It was such a vision – and only such a vision – that could render a death blow to human weaknesses like "fornication, theft, murder, adultery, avarice, wickedness, deceit, licentiousness, envy, slander, pride, folly." (Matthew 7:21-22) The centre of this new vision is not a theory, but a person: Jesus, Son of God.

As Christians, then, we are to be loyal to the vision Christ has given us; otherwise, we fail God and fail people.

⌒֎⌒

1. Give an example of sacrificing something important for the greater good.
2. Why is it so important to follow the spirit of the law rather than the letter of the law?
3. What does James mean in the second reading when he tells us to be "doers of the word and not merely hearers"?
4. Both the good and the bad come from within the human heart. Reflect on this truth.

Twenty-third Sunday in Ordinary Time

Isaiah 35:4-7
James 2:1-5
Mark 7:31-37

Be Strong, Do Not Fear!

It is difficult to live out our faith journey in today's world. Everywhere we turn, we are told that only material things matter. We need encouragement if we are to continue on the path of faith – and lots of it. This Sunday's readings give us just that.

In the first reading, Isaiah addresses the discouraged people of Israel as they taste their first bitter days of exile in Babylon, saying, "Be strong, do not fear!" He continues, "Here is your God.... He will come and save you. Then the eyes of the blind shall be opened, and the ears of the deaf unstopped.... For waters shall break forth in the wilderness, and streams in the desert."

In the second reading, James warns the members of his community not to make distinctions between classes of people, treating the poor badly and the rich favourably. Doing so would make them "judges with evil thoughts." God judges by what is in the heart, not what is in the pocket. Indeed, if anyone is to be favoured, James contends, it is the poor and the lonely. For "has not God chosen the poor in the world to be rich in faith and to be heirs of the kingdom that he has promised to those who love him?"

In the gospel, Mark notes that Jesus left Jewish soil and travelled into the Gentile regions surrounding the Sea of Galilee. While there, "a deaf man who had an impediment in his speech" was brought to him. Jesus took the man aside, "put his fingers into his ears, and he spat and touched his tongue. Then looking up to heaven, he sighed and said to him, 'Ephphatha,' that is, 'Be opened.' And immediately his ears were opened, his tongue was released, and he spoke plainly."

God's graciousness was not only for the Jewish people, but for all humanity. To all people Jesus offers the richness of divine life. He opens our ears so that we may hear his voice, loosens our tongues so that we may proclaim his word, and heals our paralysis so that we may walk in his ways. In Jesus, Isaiah's words come true: "For waters shall break forth in the wilderness, and streams in the desert...."

Thus we can stand firm against the many voices of materialism that surround us and not think of giving up our journey of faith. For God, through the risen Jesus, is within us, offering to slake our thirst with the abundant waters of eternal life. "Be strong, do not fear!"

1. Offer examples of how the world today emphasizes and encourages material gain.
2. In a sense we are all in exile, for the world confines us to its own narrow horizons. Reflect on this in light of Isaiah's words to the exiles in Babylon.
3. Jesus cured a Gentile man who was deaf and mute. How does Jesus open our ears to hear and loose our tongues to speak?
4. What word or phrase from the readings will you carry with you this week?

Twenty-fourth Sunday in Ordinary Time

Isaiah 50:5-9
James 2:14-18
Mark 8:27-35

Death and Taxes

We live in a society that provides many services – health care, education, good roads and so much more. How do we pay for all this? Through taxes. Every dollar earned, every purchase made, every service rendered results in tax revenue to foot the bill.

Do we pay a kind of tax for being Christian? This Sunday's readings shed some light on this question.

In the first reading, Isaiah speaks out in the name of all Israel: "I gave my back to those who struck me, and my cheeks to those who pulled out the beard; I did not hide my face from insult and spitting."

Isaiah knew that there was a price to pay for belonging to God's people, and that price involved suffering. Yet he also knew that even so, the price was low. Besides, as he says, "The Lord God helps me…he who vindicates me is near. Who will contend with me? Let us stand up together…. It is the Lord God who helps me."

In the second reading, James sets the stage for the gospel. He recognizes that to be a true Christian, one must engage in good works. He writes, "So faith by itself, if it has no works, is dead." Good works demand time, effort and self-sacrifice. That's the price.

In the gospel, Jesus asks his followers, "Who do people say that I am?" They tell him what several other people say. Then Jesus asks pointedly, "But who do you say that I am?" Peter answers in the name of all: "You are the Messiah."

Immediately, Jesus points out that he himself "must undergo great suffering...be rejected...and be killed." This didn't go over well with Peter, and he said so. Jesus rebuked him, and then said, "If any want to become my followers, let them deny themselves and take up their cross and follow me. For those who want to save their life will lose it."

The cross (love for God and neighbour above all else) is thus the price we must pay for being Christian. Yet the price is not too high. For, as Jesus promises, "Those who lose their life for my sake, and for the sake of the gospel, will save it."

1. When have you had to pay a price for being honest or for sticking to your principles?
2. Why is the cross not too high a price for us to pay?
3. Reflect on the reward Jesus promises to those who follow him.
4. What word or phrase from the readings will you carry with you this week?

Twenty-fifth Sunday in Ordinary Time

Wisdom 2:12, 17-20
James 3:16–4:3
Mark 9:30-37

A Tale of Two Wisdoms

There are two kinds of wisdom. The first is the worldly kind. It can be described best by certain phrases like "getting ahead in the world," "climbing the ladder of success," "being number one," "being top dog." In effect, the centre of worldly wisdom is "I." And "I" ought to get ahead of everyone else – make more money, acquire more goods, climb higher and higher up the social and executive ladders. Spirits may be crushed in the process, or moral rules transgressed. No matter.

The other kind of wisdom is vastly different. Though called "godly wisdom," it is far closer to the human heart than is worldly wisdom. And best of all, it has an immeasurably richer outcome. There is an excellent description of these two kinds of wisdom in the readings for this Sunday.

The first reading sharply depicts the heart of the worldly wise. They say to themselves, as the Book of Wisdom attests, "Let us lie in wait for the righteous one, who makes life inconvenient to us...let us test him with insult and torture...[and] condemn him to a shameful death." Those who live only by worldly wisdom instinctively hate the godly wise, for the lives of good people show up the malice in their own worldly hearts.

In the second reading, James clearly contrasts the two types of wisdom. "Where there is envy and selfish ambition, there will also be disorder and wickedness of every kind. But the wisdom from above is first pure, then peaceable, gentle, willing to yield, full of mercy and good fruits, without a trace of partiality or hypocrisy."

In the gospel, the two wisdoms clash. Jesus sees where the worldly wisdom of the religious and political leaders is leading. So he says to his followers, "The Son of Man is to be betrayed into human hands, and they will kill him, and three days after being killed, he will rise again."

In doing his Father's will, Jesus meets the selfish aims of the religious and political leaders head on. The cross is the result of that clash, but victory belongs to Jesus and comes to all those who follow him.

1. Have you ever been ridiculed by the worldly wise because of your faith?
2. What does the second reading say about "the wisdom from above"?
3. In the gospel, the apostles were using "worldly wisdom" in arguing about who was the greatest. How did Jesus correct them?
4. What word or phrase from the readings will you carry with you this week?

Twenty-sixth Sunday in Ordinary Time

Numbers 11:16a, 17c, 25-29
James 5:1-6
Mark 9:38-43, 45, 47-48

The Changing Face of the Church

The face of the Church is changing. It used to be largely clerical; now it is becoming increasingly lay – not so much in terms of numbers, since the laity have always been more numerous, but rather in terms of ministry. Today, more and more, the laity are accepting the challenge to exercise their baptismal call as ministers in the Church.

Are lay people stepping out of line, taking over from priests and religious? Not if we take seriously the readings for this Sunday.

In the first reading, Moses, who is unable to carry the whole load of leadership, appealed to God. So God "took some of the spirit that was on Moses and put it on the seventy elders. When the Spirit rested upon them, they prophesied." Eldad and Medad were not present for the sharing, but they also began to prophesy. Some people objected. But Moses answered, "Would that all the Lord's people were prophets, and that the Lord would put his spirit on them!"

The same sort of situation arises in the gospel. Someone outside the circle of Jesus' followers was performing miracles in Jesus' name. The disciples tried to stop him. But Jesus said, "Do not stop him; for no one who does a deed of power in my name will be able soon afterward to speak evil of me."

It is clear then. Ministry is not to be confined to the few – it is the preserve of all. Jesus put it very concretely in the gospel when he said, "For truly I tell you, whoever gives you a cup of water to drink because you bear the name of Christ will by no means lose the reward."

This does not mean that the role of leadership in the Church is being threatened. Leadership is an integral part of the Church. But what is leadership? It is a matter of serving others. Part of that service is encouraging and enabling the laity to exercise their gifts.

1. Today's laity are more knowledgeable about the Christian faith and more ready to serve than in the past. How has this changed the face of the Church in your area?

2. A prophet is someone who speaks and acts in God's name. How can lay people be prophets?

3. Reflect on how Jesus was open to anyone who performed deeds in his name, and how he commended the smallest deed done for others.

4. What word or phrase from the readings will you carry with you this week?

Twenty-seventh Sunday in Ordinary Time

Genesis 2:7ab, 8b, 18-24
Hebrews 2:9-11
Mark 10:2-16

The Key Ingredient

No matter how carefully you bake a cake, it won't turn out right if you neglect to add a key ingredient.

Marriage, of course, is no piece of cake, but I believe that many marriages fail because they are missing a key ingredient. This key ingredient has to do with the relationship of married couples to the Creator.

God made human beings in his own image. He set them as his regents to oversee material creation and commanded them, "Be fruitful and multiply, and fill the earth and subdue it." (Genesis 1:28) (To subdue creation means to transform it, to humanize it.) This divine command is essential in the making of a marriage. God made humans, male and female, to be partners in creation. In the first reading for this Sunday, we read, "It is not good that the man should be alone; I will make him a helper as his partner." After God had done so, man exclaimed, "This at last is bone of my bones and flesh of my flesh." The reading concludes with these covenantal words: "Therefore a man leaves his father and his mother and clings to his wife, and they become one flesh."

Man and woman are thus joined to one another in a covenant. They are to be one in body, mind, and soul. Together they also have a covenant with God, cooperating with God in bringing creation to fulfillment. The two covenants go together. One cannot be fulfilled apart from the other.

In the gospel, Jesus reminds us of this covenant ideal as found in Genesis. When the Jews mentioned how Moses had allowed them to divorce, Jesus said, "Because of your hardness of heart he wrote this commandment for you. But from the beginning of creation, 'God made them male and female'...therefore what God has joined together, let no one separate." Those who do separate and remarry, Jesus says, commit adultery.*

In the second reading, the author of the letter to the Hebrews reminds us that Jesus is "now crowned with glory and honour because of the suffering of death, so that by the grace of God he might taste death for everyone." All of us – married or single – are called upon to die to self by loving God and our neighbour above all else. This is the covenant challenge.

1. Reflect on the dignity of marriage, keeping in mind its origins and the Church's teaching that marriage has two equal purposes – being open to new life and growing together in mutual love.
2. What pressures do married couples face today?
3. How can Christian marriages be strengthened?
4. What word or phrase from the readings will you carry with you this week?

* Jesus' words seem to rule out divorce. However, some people enter marriage without realizing its true nature, or have no intention of living up to the marriage bond. In these and other cases, there is no true marriage, and an annulment can be sought by those married in the Roman Catholic Church.

Twenty-eighth Sunday
in Ordinary Time

Wisdom 7:7-11
Hebrews 4:12-13
Mark 10:17-30

The Wisdom of Solomon

Help! The dollar sign is fast becoming the dominant sign of value. What a tragedy! Who can teach us the true values of life? Who better than the God who made us, as we discover in the readings for this Sunday.

In the first reading, Solomon prays for wisdom. His prayer is heard, and he receives the gift of wisdom. He then becomes ecstatic and voices his pleasure at such a treasure. "I preferred her to sceptres and thrones, and I accounted wealth as nothing in comparison with her. Neither did I liken to her any priceless gem, because all gold is but a little sand in her sight, and silver will be accounted as clay before her. I loved her more than health and beauty."

What is wisdom? How do we acquire it? The second reading and the gospel give us some direction.

"Indeed the word of God is living and active," the author of Hebrews explains, "sharper than any two-edged sword...before God no creature is hidden, but all are naked and laid bare to the eyes of the one to whom we must render an account."

Wisdom is thus closely associated with God and with the word of God. It is associated with God because to acquire it we must pray, as the first reading tells us. Then, as the second reading makes clear, we are to listen to the word of God, not only with our ears but also with our hearts. Only then will wisdom become "alive and active" within us, enabling us to know what is truly valuable and what is not.

In the gospel, a rich man asks Jesus how he can obtain eternal life. Jesus tells him to keep the commandments. When the rich man says he has done so from his youth, "Jesus, looking at him, loved him and said, 'You lack one thing; go, sell what you own, and give the money to the poor, and you will have treasure in heaven; then come, follow me.'"

For the rich man, such a challenge was too high a price to pay. The coins in his purse jingled too loudly and his heart was too selfish. He preferred his present riches to a future life of supreme happiness.

The apostles, on the other hand, left everything and followed Jesus. They put him first in their lives. Jesus promised them, and all who follow him, a hundredfold reward in this life and in the next, in eternal life.

Thus we discover true wisdom in God's own Son. If we accept Jesus, the whole world is ours. If we refuse him, we end up with nothing.

1. How is the almighty dollar taking over our value system?
2. Reflect on Solomon's praise of wisdom in the first reading.
3. How is the word of God "living and active," as the author of Hebrews claims?
4. Contrast the rich man's reaction to Jesus' words with that of the apostles.

Twenty-ninth Sunday
in Ordinary Time

Isaiah 53:4, 10-11
Hebrews 4:14-16
Mark 10:35-45

Shortcuts

Some shortcuts are good – on a trip, we can avoid busy areas and save time by taking a shortcut. But when it comes to human maturity, shortcuts do not work. We cannot jump from infancy to adulthood. We have to go through all the stages of the growth process.

In a similar way, growing up as Christians allows for no shortcuts. This Sunday's readings bring home this point.

In the first reading, Isaiah speaks of the growing pains of Israel. Personifying Israel, he says: "It was the will of the Lord to crush him [Israel] with pain." But "When you make his life an offering for sin, he shall...prolong his days...my servant shall make many righteous."

Isaiah recognized that the sufferings of Israel would lead to its maturity. What is more, it will be these very sufferings, patiently accepted, that will justify "many" (for "many," we can read "all").

In the second reading, the author of the letter to the Hebrews makes the point that Jesus himself did not take any shortcuts to glory. He went through what we humans go through. "For we do not have a high priest [Jesus] who is unable to sympathize with our weaknesses, but we have one who in every respect has been tested as we are, yet without sin."

Jesus submitted totally to our human condition. He was like us in all things except personal sin. For sin, unlike temptation, is the repudiation of God. It undermines our true humanity.

The gospel reading tells us how the disciples James and John were looking for a spiritual shortcut. They wanted to occupy the seats on Jesus' right hand when he came to glory. But Jesus knew that it could not be that easy. So he said to them, "Are you able to drink the cup that I drink, or be baptized with the baptism that I am baptized with?"

Jesus was telling James and John (and all of us) that there is only one way to glory – the way of love. This kind of love accepts whatever suffering may come, even death itself. Jesus concludes by saying that all who follow him must be willing to serve others. "For the Son of Man came not to be served but to serve, and to give his life as a ransom for many."

We must not look for shortcuts on the Christian way. There are none. There is only a straight and narrow path – giving ourselves in loving service to God and our neighbour. By taking this path we and those we influence will share more fully in the abundance of God's love.

1. Describe a shortcut you once took that didn't work out.
2. Share the pains and heartaches you've had that turned out to be blessings.
3. Reflect on the true humanity of Jesus.
4. How are we to "drink the cup" and "be baptized" with the baptism that Jesus accepted?

Thirtieth Sunday in Ordinary Time

Jeremiah 31:7-9
Hebrews 5:1-6
Mark 10:46-52

God Keeps up the Pursuit

When we truly love people, we do not easily give up on them. We keep reaching out to them, hoping that they will come back to us.

God doesn't give up on us, either. God's efforts are far more compassionate, constant and effective than ours could ever be. God's loving pursuit is the theme of this Sunday's readings.

In the first reading, Jeremiah assures the Jews living in the northern part of Israel that God had not abandoned them, and never will. They had just been ravaged by the fierce Assyrians and their kingdom was no more. But, in God's name, Jeremiah gives them words of hope: "See, I am going to bring them from the land of the north, and gather them from the farthest parts of the earth, among them those who are blind and those who are lame...for I have become a father to Israel."

The second reading, continuing the theme of last Sunday, assures us that in Jesus we have a compassionate high priest. "Every high priest chosen from among mortals is put in charge of things pertaining to God.... He is able to deal gently with the ignorant and wayward, since he himself is subject to weakness." Christ is just such a high priest, one who deals with us gently, never giving up on us.

In the gospel, Jesus cures Bartimaeus, a blind man. Many in the crowd scolded Bartimaeus for being so pushy. They told him to back off. But he would not.

He kept calling out, "Jesus, Son of David, have mercy on me!"

Jesus stopped and said, "Call him here.... What do you want me to do for you?" Bartimaeus replied, "My teacher, let me see again." Jesus assured him, "Go; your faith has made you well."

In this way God cares for us, no matter who we are or what we've done. God never abandons anyone, even those who abandon him. God loves us and will continue to pursue us whenever we stray. God will never ever give up. His loving arms will always be open, eager to embrace us. This is cause for great rejoicing!

1. Think of a time when someone you loved reached out to you during a difficult period in your life. How did this make you feel?
2. Reflect on some of the reasons why people stray from God. What leads them back to God?
3. What does it mean to you to know that God will always reach out to you and welcome you with open arms?
4. What word or phrase from the readings will you carry with you this week?

Thirty-first Sunday in Ordinary Time

Deuteronomy 6:2-6
Hebrews 7:23-28
Mark 12:28-34

Putting It All Together

Today we live in a very complex world. Life used to be simpler – people were caught up mostly with their immediate neighbourhood, and the outside world was far away. Now, however, thanks to the media, the whole world comes crowding into our lives. All the world's problems are at our doorstep.

Amidst all this complexity, how do we put it all together? The readings for this Sunday point the way.

After receiving the Ten Commandments from God and delivering them to the people, Moses directs them to see to it that "you and your children and your children's children may fear the Lord your God all the days of your life, and keep all his decrees and his commandments." Then Moses sums up all the commandments in one meaningful sentence, "You shall love the Lord your God with all your heart, and with all your soul, and with all your might." Moses is telling us that if we put God first in our lives, all will go well with us. Even in the fastest-moving world we can keep our bearings.

In the second reading, the author of the letter to the Hebrews assures us that Jesus, who "holds his priesthood permanently.... is able for all time to save those who approach God through him."

In the gospel, Jesus repeats the command Moses gave about loving God above all else. He then adds a further command, "You shall love your neighbour as yourself," and concludes, "There is no other commandment greater than these." Notice how the word "commandment" is singular. That means the love of God and neighbour are one command. We cannot love God without loving our neighbour.

How, then, do we go about putting it all together? We don't! God does. But we have a key role to play. By loving God and our neighbour above all else, we do our part in a complex world. God takes our seemingly small efforts and fits them into the picture of the emerging "new heavens and new earth." Only God can do this work, but our lives in God are an important part of the picture.

1. How has the speed of the world around you changed over the past 10 (or 20 or 50) years?
2. The reverse side of a tapestry seems to be a mishmash of strings going every which way. There's no clear pattern. The right side reveals a beautiful pattern where everything makes sense. How is life today something like that?
3. What does the Christian faith tell us about our evolving humanity and our evolving universe?
4. How can love for God and our neighbour result in a better world?

Thirty-second Sunday
in Ordinary Time

1 Kings 17:10-16
Hebrews 9:24-28
Mark 12:38-44

Secularization

We are often warned that "secularization" poses a serious threat to our Christian faith. What is secularization and how can we counteract it?

The word itself comes from the word "secular," which in turn comes from a Latin word meaning "of this age." Secularization reduces all values to worldly ones. It does not acknowledge the higher values that come from God.

The way secularization works is very subtle. Its main arena is the media, which are largely controlled by the dollar sign. Hence what we read and hear, day in and day out, are not the values revealed by God but the secular values of this world. Such values do not and cannot satisfy our deepest longings. Hence a purely secular society is bound to fail. We live, as Jesus taught, "by every word that comes from the mouth of God." (Matthew 4:4)

How do we resist the pull of secularization? This Sunday's readings offer some advice.

In the first reading, the widow of Zarephath gives food to the prophet Elijah even though it means near starvation for herself and son. Such charity doesn't make economic sense! It makes God-sense, however, and the widow is richly rewarded.

The gospel is also about a generous widow, who gives a coin to the Temple, one she surely needed. Her generosity was noted by Jesus. We can be sure that she, too, was richly deserving in God's eyes.

The second reading, from the letter to the Hebrews, is about generosity as well – the generosity of Christ, the greatest of high priests. He gave his life on the cross so that we might be freed from enslavement to sin. Christ will return to reward all who live by God's values, not by secular ones.

The readings for this Sunday encourage us to resist secularization and live more fully, and eternally, by the much deeper values of faith.

1. Where do you see evidence of secularization around you? How has it affected your own life?
2. What values are exemplified by the two widows in this Sunday's readings?
3. Reflect on the values Jesus lived by, especially those that prompted him to give his life for us.
4. What word or phrase from the readings will you carry with you this week?

Thirty-third Sunday in Ordinary Time

Daniel 12:1-3
Hebrews 10:11-14, 18
Mark 13:24-32

The Far Sight

Our world is so caught up in the present that it is increasingly difficult for us to think of the future, especially the ultimate future. But God and the Church urge us to open our minds and be far-sighted.

The three readings for this Sunday are concerned with "the Far Sight."

In the first reading, the prophet Daniel, speaking about the end of time, says, "At that time Michael, the great prince, the protector of your people, shall arise...at that time your people shall be delivered.... Many of those who sleep in the dust of the earth shall awake, some to everlasting life, and some to shame and ever-lasting contempt. Those who are wise shall shine like the brightness of the sky...like the stars forever and ever." These are comforting words indeed!

The second reading is equally comforting. When Christ, our high priest, "had offered for all time a single sacrifice for sins, 'he sat down at the right hand of God,' and since then has been waiting 'until his enemies would be made a footstool for his feet.'" In doing so, the author continues, "he has perfected for all time those who are sanctified."

In the gospel, Jesus quotes the prophets of old speaking about the last days of the world, then contin-ues: "Then they will see 'the Son of Man coming in clouds' with great power and glory." He warns his followers to remember this as they go about their daily lives. When will these last days come? At any time,

Jesus implies, but as to the exact day and hour, "no one knows, neither the angels in heaven, nor the Son, but only the Father."

This, then, is "the Far Sight." By accepting it and living it we shape our present lives. For the end-time is a present force as well as a future hope. It allows us to put the passing things of this world into perspective and use them as building blocks for the future. By God's grace we will become people who live by "the Far Sight."

~❁~

1. Give some examples of how our world is caught up in the present.
2. What does it mean to work out of a vision of life?
3. How does the end of time, as outlined in the readings, affect our present lives?
4. What word or phrase from the readings will you carry with you this week?

Christ the King

Daniel 7:13-14
Revelation 1:5-8
John 18:33b-37

Truth Is Power

We sometimes shiver when we hear the word
"power." Most of us, I dare say, have suffered from its
abuse at one time or another. We may have been
victims of physical power, browbeaten by intellectual
power, or made to suffer from psychological power.
Such abuse of power is sad. Fortunately, there is
good power, benign power, health-giving and soul-
strengthening power. The readings for this final Sunday in the liturgical year, the feast of Christ the King,
make this clear.

The words of the first reading, from the book of the
prophet Daniel, were written in the middle of the
second century BCE. Through his words, the author
intended to encourage the Jewish people, who were
being persecuted by their Greek overlords. Daniel shares
the following vision with them:

...I saw one like a human being
coming with the clouds of heaven.
And he came to the Ancient One
and was presented before him.
To him was given dominion
and glory and kingship,
that all peoples, nations and languages
should serve him.

The early Christians realized that Daniel's prophecy was fulfilled in Jesus. Through Jesus' life, death
and resurrection, he was given power over all creation.

In the second reading, the book of Revelation refers to Jesus as "the faithful witness, the firstborn of the dead, and the ruler of the kings of the earth."

The gospel indicates the kind of power that Jesus wielded. Standing before Pilate, Jesus is asked if he is a king. He replies, "You say that I am a king. For this was I born, and for this I came into the world, to testify to the truth. Everyone who belongs to the truth listens to my voice."

Jesus thus gives us a deep insight into what real power is all about. He makes clear that the highest power is not physical, not legalistic. The highest power is the power of truth. Real power is knowing and living the truth about human life. And that is what Jesus taught us. Indeed, he himself is "the way, and the truth and the life." In Jesus, then, we possess this truth, possessing it in him, we are assured of gaining victory over evil and inheriting eternal life.

1. From your own experience, give examples of the abuse of power and of the proper, life-giving use of power.

2. How do you see the power of truth at work?

3. Though most of us do not have a lot of financial or legal power, we do have Christ-power. What does this mean in your life?

4. What word or phrase from the readings will you carry with you this week?

The Living with Christ Sunday Missal

A personal copy of the *Living with Christ Sunday Missal* helps Catholics prepare for and participate more fully in the Sunday liturgy. Contains complete readings and mass texts, as well as selected hymns, for all Sundays and feast days. The perfect companion to *Preparing for Sunday!*

Fr. John Spicer CSsR is the director of the Adult Learning Commission of the Archdiocese of Edmonton, Alberta. He is a well-known and frequent contributor to the Catholic press, especially in western Canada. His *Preparing for Sunday* series continues with separate volumes for Years A and C.